M. S. RANDHAWA

KANGRA PAINTINGS ON LOVE

NATIONAL MUSEUM, NEW DELHI

Kangra Paintings on Love is the second in the series of five monographs on Kangra Paintings planned by Dr. M. S. Randhawa. The first was *Kangra Paintings of the Bhāgavata Purāṇa*. The next in the series will be *Kangra Paintings of Jayadeva's Gīta Govinda*.

Layout and Book Design
J. Bhattacharjee

Colour Plates 26. Text Illustrations 89

Sole Distributors
The Publications Division
Minijtry of Information & Broadcasting
Old Secretariat, DELHI-6.

First Published 1962

Published by the National Museum, New Delhi, and printed by Isaac N. Isaac, at Vakil & Sons (Private) Limited, Narandas Building, Sprott Road, 18 Ballard Estate, Bombay, India.

To

IQBAL

When one writes about Woman, one must steep one's pen in the colours of the rainbow, and scatter the dust from butterflies' wings on the page. With every movement of one's hand a pearl must fall.

Diderot
Sur les femmes

FOREWORD

It is not surprising that the finest expressions of art centre round the basic facts of life, for what is more familiar and yet mysterious than birth, life and death? From immemorial times, man has sought to understand their meaning, and when logical terms fail to explain them, has resorted to their embodiment in music and dance, poetry and painting, sculpture and architecture.

A special characteristic of Indian art has been the fusion of the material and the spiritual in all artistic endeavour. Contrary to popular belief, the ascetic ideal has moulded only certain marginal groups in India. The vast majority have sought a life in which the secular and the religious have influenced one another, and made spiritual realisation concrete, and mundane experiences religious. In the words of the Vaishṇava poet, the beloved has become divine, and Divinity has become the beloved.

The Kangra paintings on love, represented in this volume, are true to this basic tradition of India. They deal with love in all its fulness and yet there is always in the background a sense of unrevealed spiritual truths. The portraits are of full-blooded men and women who delight in passionate love, but there is always a glimpse of the unearthly, even in the midst of their physical ecstasy.

The Kangra paintings grew out of the courtly art of the Mughals, but underwent a radical change in the lovely valleys under the shadow of the Himalayas. In a setting, where life was unsophisticated, and men and women lived much closer to nature, the highly sophisticated art of the royal courts gained a new softness, delicacy, and human feeling.

The Kangra Paintings on Love is the second of five monographs, in which Dr. M. S. Randhawa proposes to cover the best paintings of the Kangra school, including many which are preserved in the National Museum itself.

The first monograph, on the *Bhāgavata Purāṇa*, has already won many admirers, and the second will add to the delight and joy of many more readers in India and abroad. Dr. Randhawa has earned our gratitude for the love and care with which he is editing and publishing this series on behalf of the National Museum, New Delhi.

New Delhi
17th July, 1961

Humayun Kabir
Union Minister for Scientific Research and Cultural Affairs

PREFACE

In July 1958, I suggested to Mr. Humayun Kabir, Union Minister for Scientific Research and Cultural Affairs, that the National Museum should bring out a series of monographs on Indian painting, in which the master works of Indian painters may be published for the education, enlightenment and pleasure of art lovers. It was also felt that a publication programme of this nature would provide an opportunity for publishing the best paintings in the collection of the National Museum. I proposed that the study of the Kangra paintings under this series be entrusted to me. This suggestion was accepted by Mr. Kabir, and accordingly a programme of publications was drawn up in consultation with Dr. K. N. Puri, Assistant Director, National Museum, and Mr. C. Sivaramamurti, Keeper, National Museum. I agreed to deal with Kangra painting in five monographs so as to cover the best paintings of the Kangra School. The first monograph, *Kangra Paintings of the Bhāgavata Purāṇa*, has just been published, and the present monograph on the *Śṛiṅgāra* paintings is the second in the series.

The term 'Kangra Paintings' which has been adopted as the title of this book has been used in the broader sense. It refers not only to the art of painting which developed in the Kangra Valley at Guler, and Nurpur and Tira-Sujanpur, and Alampur and Nadaun — the places connected with Maharaja Sansar Chand — but also includes paintings done in similar style in Garhwal, Chamba, Jammu, Mandi, Suket, Bilaspur, Baghal and other Hill States in the Western Himalayas. No doubt the paintings from all these States have certain individual characteristics, but they have the same spirit, which gives a particular character and flavour to Kangra art and distinguishes it from its Mughal predecessor. Moreover, if the choice of paintings had been confined to the paintings from the States of Kangra and Guler only, which constitute the Kangra style *strictu sensu*, it would not have been possible to illustrate the various situations described in the *Rasikapriyā*.

In this book, I have given major findings of recent research on Kangra paintings, which are generally accepted by scholars who are interested in this subject. No doubt, there are differences of opinion on details, but these, I felt, are so insignificant that they are best left alone. Otherwise, the book would have acquired a controversial air, which is best avoided in a work of art, particularly in this one, which deals with the theme of love.

This book mainly deals with the *Rasikapriyā* of Keshav Dās, though there is a reference to the works of some other Hindi poets and rhetoricians also. It is for the first time that a free translation of the text of the *Rasikapriyā* has been provided. What impresses one is the manner and thoroughness with which the Hindi poets have analysed the feelings of woman towards man in particular situations and circumstances. What intimate knowledge of the passions of the body and soul is revealed in this analysis? It still holds good even in the modern world with changed environment, and most women, even of the present age, fall in one category or the other of the *Nāyikās* described by Keshav Dās. Mixed with an intellectual urge for analysis and codification was a preference for enumeration. This was perhaps very necessary in an age when printing presses were not known, and reliance was largely on memory for recital of poetry. The *Rasikapriyā* was written for the enjoyment of princes and the aristocracy in the late 16th century. As the writers were men, naturally they made woman the subject of their study and paid much less attention to their own sex. Possibly woman is also much more interesting than man, and it is her study and inspiration, which is the source of most of the literatures of the world.

In the 18th century, the text of the *Rasikapriyā* was selected by artists for purposes of illustration for the delectation of their royal patrons, the Rajas of the Hill States of the Punjab. For the enjoyment of a work of art, it is necessary not only to know the name of the artist who produced it, but also what the people were like, for whom it was created, and what their feelings, mode of thought and way of looking at the world were. This art blossomed under the inspiration of Vaishṇavism which was the religion of the Hindus, and thus we find that Kangra painting is not a sudden development, but is the culmination of a spiritual and literary revival. It was a puritanical society with a strict moral code, particularly in regard to sex, and women were kept in seclusion by the practice of *purdah*. The inference drawn that this art, the central theme of which is love, developed under such conditions as an escape cannot be regarded as far-fetched.

In the task of translating the text from the *Rasikapriyā*, I received great help from my friend and colleague S. D. Bhambri, an eminent Hindi scholar. In fact the main burden of translation work was on his shoulders, and in spite of heavy official work, he cheerfully assisted me. I had an invaluable helper in Prem Nath, who also prepared the index. P. Banerjee and Krishan Kumar read the proofs. D. N. Paliwal was also of great help in the translation of some of the Hindi texts. This translation will be of value not only in the study of Kangra paintings, but will also unlock the secrets of the Rajasthani paintings, a large series of which are based on the themes from the *Rasikapriyā*. I also express my gratitude to Calcutta University for permission to quote from the works of Dineshchandra Sen, of which they hold copyright.

The layout and book design have been prepared by J. Bhattacharjee, and the cover design by N. S. Bisht. Fram Poonawala of Commercial Art Engravers (Private) Ltd. prepared excellent blocks of the paintings, and G. U. Mehta, Managing Director and S. M. Desai of Vakil & Sons (Private) Ltd. took personal interest in its printing and production. V. P. Agnihotri, Under Secretary of the Ministry of Scientific Research and Cultural Affairs, gave unstinted support to this project which saved administrative delays. Above all, W. G. Archer, the most eminent scholar of Indian Painting, has been my constant friend and guide, and grudged nothing from his marvellous store of learning and knowledge of Kangra paintings. I have benefited greatly from his friendly criticism and the numerous suggestions, which he gave.

I also express my sincere gratitude for the hard work put in by my Personal Assistants, S. Viswanathan, Satya Paul and L. Rajagopalan, in typing the manuscript as a labour of love. I further express my gratitude to Mr. Humayun Kabir, Minister for Scientific

Research and Cultural Affairs, Government of India, and Dr. Grace Morley, Director, National Museum, for the personal interest they have taken in this publication.

The most difficult task in producing this book was the collection of paintings from the Museums and Art Galleries in different cities of India as well as from the collections of private collectors. Most of the paintings have never been reproduced before, and are new material for study of Kangra art. What an effort it was to explore these collections can hardly be described! It meant travel of thousands of miles over a period of ten years to the remotest places from Chamba, Jammu, Mandi, Bilaspur, Arki, Haripur-Guler and Lambagraon in the Punjab Himalayas to the cities of Lucknow, Allahabad, Varanasi, Patna, Calcutta and Bombay. What was much more difficult was to induce the private collectors to show their paintings and ultimately to part with them for reproduction. This no doubt made me conscious of the trust they all reposed in me by parting with their paintings for months, which they had never even shown to anyone but the trusted members of their families. I express my gratitude to the officers in charge of the National Museum, New Delhi; Bhārat Kalā Bhavan, Varanasi; Municipal Museum, Allahabad; State Museum, Lucknow; Punjab Museum, Patiala; Indian Museum, Calcutta; Asutosh Museum of Indian Art, University of Calcutta, Calcutta and Dogra Art Gallery, Jammu, for the loan of their paintings. Apart from the museums in India some of the museums in England and the U.S.A. also cooperated. I express my thanks to the Directors of the Victoria and Albert Museum and the British Museum, London; the Museum of Fine Arts, Boston, and the Cleveland Museum of Art, Cleveland, Ohio, for allowing the use of photographs of some of the masterpieces of Kangra paintings in their collections. The finest Kangra paintings are in the collection of Raja Dhruv Dev Chand of Lambagraon, who is a descendant of Maharaja Sansar Chand. I am deeply indebted to him for the loan of several of his paintings. On a visit to Jammu in April, 1960, one of the pleasant surprises was to see a collection of masterpieces from Guler in the palace of Yuvraj Karan Singh. On a request made, he not only gave on loan one of his finest paintings for reproduction, but freely permitted photographing of his collections out of which quite a number have been used in the introductory chapters of this book. I also express my gratitude to Seth Kasturbhai Lalbhai of Ahmedabad, Shrimati Sumati Morarjee and Shri Jagmohandas K. Modi of Bombay, and Seth Gopi Krishna Kanoria of Calcutta, for the loan of their paintings for reproduction.

The last painting to be collected was 'Tryst in the Forest' (Plate XVIII). I happened to pay a visit to Varanasi in December, 1960. When my work was over, I thought of meeting Miss Alice Boner, an artist and scholar, who has been living at Assi Ghat in Varanasi for many years. Next morning, I was taken to her lovely home overlooking the Gaṅgā by Anand Krishen. While waiting for her in her study, admiring the sculptures, and the sight of boats plying in the river, my eye wandered to a painting hanging on the wall. On close examination, it turned out to be a Kangra masterpiece. On a request made to Miss Boner, she agreed to give it for reproduction.

Thus ended my quest for paintings for this book. It was relatively successful in the sense that nearly all the Kangra masterpieces from museums as well as private collections were obtained on loan. The difficulty arose only in regard to private collections. Fortunately most of the collectors, with a few exceptions, happened to be enlightened persons who were conscious of the fact that paintings are not merely precious and rare commodities meant to be cornered and concealed. They also realised that paintings reproduced in books live for a longer period. I also reminded some of them of many Kangra masterpieces, which cornered in this manner, have perished, eaten up by white ants or became casualties of weather, and this was indeed a national loss.

If you want to enjoy these paintings, sweep your mind clean of all preconceived notions and prejudices. Unlike the classical art of the West, it is not realistic art whose object was to copy Nature or to produce an illusion of natural effect. The object of this art was not realistic portrayal of human beings, nor the study of human anatomy. Its aim and object was to capture the essence of human joy and sorrow. That is why it has a peculiar technique of its own. A characteristic which these paintings share with the art of Iran is that there are no cast shadows, and the colours are pure and luminous. Above all, it is an art of the line, and the line is lyrical. It is an art, as Laurence Binyon remarks, "like a song that sings itself." There is joy not only in the faces of the lovers but in their every gesture. There is joy in the atmosphere itself, in the singing birds and in the faces of the servant girls and companions, who watch the progress of the love of the pair, often portrayed as Rādhā and Kṛishṇa. Running through these paintings is a lively sense of drama. As you see them again and again, these miniatures grow upon you and seem to possess you. They no doubt represent the finest expression of the spirit of man. As they are sincere expressions of human feelings with what spontaneous delight we respond to them!

With the march of time countries change, and nations rise and fall. Nations, which once controlled the destinies of others, stand humbled. Kings and dynasties tumble down and presidents and politicians, who are repositories of power, are lost and forgotten in the mists of time. Men, who were strutting about, drunk with power, sink into oblivion and turn into dust. The din of politics, the tumults of wars and revolutions die and are forgotten. It is the truths of science and fragrance of art which long survive the material conditions of life. Of the arts of mankind, Kangra paintings on the theme of *śṛiṅgāra* have undoubtedly an abiding place in the world's inheritance of beauty, and they will continue to delight people for they deal with the eternal theme of human love. As the Japanese poet says:

"What does never change,
Since the days of the gods,
Is the way how a river runs:
What does never change
Since the days of the gods,
Is the way how love flows."

7, Tinmurti Lane, New Delhi
April 15, 1961

M. S. Randhawa

CONTENTS

TEXT FIGURES

PLATES

Kangra Paintings on Love

Nāyaka-Nāyikā-Bheda and Bārāmāsā

CHAPTER I

KANGRA PAINTINGS ON LOVE

Śṛiṅgāra

In the middle of the 18th century A.D. when the plains of Northern India were convulsed by the invasion of Nādīr Shāh (1739), followed by the incursions of Ahmad Shāh Abdālī, a strange event took place in the Punjab hills, viz. the birth of the Kangra School of Painting at Haripur-Guler under the patronage of Raja Govardhan Chand (1744-1773), a prince with a refined taste and a passion for paintings. He gave asylum to refugee artists trained in the Mughal style of painting. In the inspiring environment of the Punjab Himalayas with their beautiful green hills, wave-like terraced paddy fields and rivulets fed with the glacial waters of the snow-covered Dhauladhar, the Mughal style with its sensitive naturalism blossomed into the Kangra style. Instead of painting flattering portraits of their masters and hunting scenes, the artists adopted themes from the love-poetry of Jayadeva, Bihārī and Keshav Dās, who wrote ecstatically of the love of Rādhā and Krishṇa. Thus developed a school of painting with a new spirit, whose artistic works are suffused with romantic love and *bhakti* mysticism.

Prakash Chand (ruled 1773-1790), the successor of Govardhan Chand, also continued the patronage of the artists, and there are a number of beautiful paintings in which his wives and children are shown. There must be a number of other paintings also, including some on love-poetry, which were painted under his patronage. He was, however, a spendthrift, and in a few years he became bankrupt. At this juncture rose a patron in the adjoining State of Kangra — Sansar Chand II (1775-1823) who attracted a number of talented artists from the court of Guler, even when he was barely 20 years of age. He was the most renowned Raja in the Kangra Valley, and was a most generous patron of the art of painting. It was under his patronage that Jayadeva's Sanskrit love-poem, the *Gīta Govinda*, Bihārī's *Satsaiyyā*, the *Bhāgavata Purāṇa*, the romantic tale of *Nala and Damayantī*, and Keshav Dās's *Rasikapriyā* and *Kavipriyā* were translated into paintings of exquisite beauty.

The first European to see the famous collection of the paintings of Maharaja Sansar Chand was Moorcroft (1820), an English traveller, a veterinary surgeon by profession, who halted at Alampur and Tira-Sujanpur as a guest of Maharaja Sansar Chand, while on his way to Yarkand, where his mission was the purchase of ponies.

The real discovery of the Kangra School of Painting we owe to Dr. A. K. Coomaraswamy, who paid a visit to Amritsar and Kangra in 1910, and obtained a large collection of these paintings from the Amritsar dealer, Radha Krishna Bharany. Coomaraswamy's first essay in the Burlington Magazine of 1910 on 'Pahari Drawings' opened a new chapter in Indian art history. Hitherto the products of the Kangra School were confused by European writers with Mughal miniatures, and it was Coomaraswamy who recognised the Hindu painting of Northern India as a distinct entity in his great work *Rajput Painting* (1916) in which he described some specimens of paintings from Rajasthan and the Punjab and Jammu hills. He not merely pointed out the significance of objects described in their historical context, but also as the expression of ideas. His writings are characterized by simplicity combined with intensity of thought, sincerity, expressiveness and aesthetic purity. As Eric Gill observes, "No other writer has written the truth in matters of art and life, and religion and piety with such wisdom and understanding." In his early writings we find sensuous joy wedded to sacredness, and he explained in a delightful manner how love which begins in the adoration of physical beauty develops into divine love, which is the essence of the teaching of Vaishṇavism. To the Western mind, which had been regarding sex as sin, on account of the Christian doctrine of original sin, and love of man for woman as love profane, as distinct from 'love divine', this interpretation must have come as a fresh breeze. He also revealed that human cultures in all their apparent diversity, are but the dialects of one and the same language of the spirit. All over the world, men are moved by similar emotions, and of these the most powerful is the affinity between the sexes, which finds expression in love.

Here it would be pertinent to refer to the work of the British orientalists who unlocked the beauty of the Sanskrit and Hindi classics to the Westerners as well as to the English educated Indians. They provided the foundation on which literature on the study of paintings has been built, and Coomaraswamy, in his *Rajput Painting*, has freely drawn on these sources. In fact, we all build upon the foundation provided by the work of our predecessors, and no person, however gifted, rises spontaneously into intellectual splendour without the parentage of antecedent thought. Of these orientalists, Sir William Jones (1792) and Sir Edwin Arnold (1875) translated into English Jayadeva's *Gīta Govinda.* F. Pincott (1897) translated Kavi Lallu Lāl's Hindi version of the *Bhāgavata Purāṇa*, known as *Prema Sāgar.* Sir George Grierson (1889) compiled information of great value on the Hindi poets, in the book entitled *The Modern Vernacular Literature of Hindustan* and also published material on the theme of *Śṛiṅgāra*, including the *Nāyaka-Nāyikā* theme based on a translation of Jaswant Singh's *Bhāshā Bhūshaṇa* along with an anthology of Bihārī Lāl's poetry.

Coomaraswamy's works inspired a number of scholars to undertake the study of Kangra Painting. O. C. Gangoly (1926) published a portfolio of paintings from the Punjab Hills as well as Rajasthan in his *Masterpieces of Rajput Painting.* He was followed by N. C. Mehta (1926), who in his *Studies in Indian Painting*, reproduced a few exquisite specimens of Kangra paintings of the *Gīta Govinda*, which he erroneously ascribed to the Tehri-Garhwal School. In 1930, J. C. French undertook his famous tour of the Punjab Himalayas and discovered a number of collections of paintings. Then followed a lull of about twenty-two years.

Fig. 1. Love divine

An event of major importance in the research and study of Kangra Painting was the publication of two important books by W. G. Archer in 1952, viz. *Indian Painting in the Punjab Hills*, followed by a monograph on *Kangra Painting* with ten reproductions in colour. Most books on Kangra paintings, published so far, had been enormously costly, printed in limited editions, and hence were accessible only to a few scholars. Archer's monograph *Kangra Painting* popularized the Kangra School in the West as well as in India. However, his collection of essays on *Indian Painting in the Punjab Hills* is very important in the sense that it was the first attempt to analyse styles and to relate them to various centres of painting in the Punjab hills. Though he had not visited the Kangra Valley, from study of styles alone, by his uncanny insight, he traced the paintings to the places where they were painted. By on-the-spot studies of various collections still in the Valley, I was able to confirm most of his findings. On account of his background of research in tribal cultures of India, he introduced the scientific method in the study of paintings, and developed a distinct technique, which apart from aesthetic appreciation of the paintings, deals with dating, provenance and study of material and social environment in which the painting developed. In addition, he probed deeper into these paintings, and pointed out the subconscious urges, which made the artists paint in the manner in which they did. The pointed cypresses, the swaying leaves of plantains, the spouts of ewers juxtaposed with vessels with *yoni*-like mouths, the play of lightning in the clouds, the twining creepers clasping the trunks of trees, and the pairs of love-birds were surely poetic symbols of the sex urge, the most fundamental of urges, which through the renewal of the rhythm of generations perpetuates the species. Above all, Archer is a critic whose poetical prose is suffused with feelings of love, and his commentaries on these paintings, characterized by aesthetic purity and joyous abandon, have delighted many who have kinship of spirit with him.

The paintings of *Nāyaka-Nāyikās*, *Bārāmāsā* and related themes are remarkable for their

Fig. 2. Companionship of love

romantic beauty, tenderness, unrestrained frankness, and complete avoidance of sentimentality. As Coomaraswamy remarks, "Rarely has any other art combined so little fear with so much tenderness, so much delight with such complete renunciation. If the Chinese have taught us best how to understand the life of Nature manifest in water and in mountains, Indian art at least can teach us how not to misunderstand desire, for we are constantly reminded here that the soul of sweet delight can never be defiled."[1]

Kangra painting glorified refinement, restraint, and divinity of beauty. Every art is a language. What the words cannot express is sometimes conveyed in painting through space enclosed in line and dabbed in colours. Kangra painting is an art both of line and colour. A vigorous rhythmical line is the basis of this art. It is also an art of colour, and the artists revelled in the use of pure blues, yellows, reds and greens. These jewel-like miniatures were executed with such care and skill that the passage of time has not dimmed their glowing colours. Being portfolio paintings, not meant to be displayed on walls, they are kept packed in pieces of cloth, and are brought out on rare occasions to be enjoyed in seclusion. This practice, no doubt, has helped in the preservation of their bright colour, which appears as fresh today as when they were painted a century and a half ago. It is an art flooded with sunlight and colour, charged with spiritual feeling, and is still strongly felt, and kindles deep emotion in the beholder. While Chinese paintings express the beauty of the mist and the mountains, the lake and the river, the willow and the cherry and the flight of birds, Kangra art is the language of human love. In a rich vocabulary of line and colour, the Kangra paintings express the emotions and the beauty of the people.

Above all, these paintings are the visual record of a culture, the warm sensuous humanism of Vaishṇavism, which found expression in poetry and ultimately in paintings of utmost delicacy and beauty. These paintings are really fossils of a culture, which, when studied and interpreted, tell us more about the historical past than the records of travellers, or the dull cataloguing of facts by the so-called historians and archivists. They mirror their age and humanity and the ideals which inspired them. Vaishṇavism which kindled the creative enthusiasm of the age preached the religion of love. The love they had in view was not the parental love of the father for his children, but the love of husband for his wife, love of a kind most intimate, ecstatic and passionate. In the Kangra Valley it inspired an art which reached the heights of joyous aesthetic harmony, which its Mughal predecessor failed to achieve. Kangra artists dealt with the eternal theme of human love expressed in the legend of Rādhā and Kṛishṇa. Whenever lovers are shown, whether in *Nāyaka-Nāyikā* or *Bārāmāsā* pictures, they are usually in the form of Rādhā and Kṛishṇa who are the ideal lovers. These are universal feelings which are shared by human beings all over the world. In their paintings of *Nāyaka-Nāyikās*, the Kangra artists pass on these feelings to us, and these are so powerfully conveyed that we are infected by them and also experience them. In this sense, Kangra art reaches the definition of Tolstoy.[2]

Fig. 3. Deep intimacy of love

Kangra art exulted in feminine beauty. The type of female beauty shown in these paintings is based not on any particular model, but on scores of women whom the artists saw in their daily life. Models for the chin, the mouth, the eye, the forehead and coiffure were provided by many women, and the artists distilled the essence of female beauty in these paintings. Thus the formulae of female beauty which we see in these paintings represent a vision, realized through the contemplation of a thousand beauties, transformed and gilded by the magic of imagination. While most European artists painted from models, e.g. Rubens used his wife as a model, Correggio his sister, and Titian his daughter, there were a few like Raphael who used the method of Kangra artists. "As beauty is rare among women, I make use of a

Fig.4. Security of love

certain ideal, which is of my own creation. However that may be, I must tell you that in order to paint one beauty, I must see several,"[3] wrote Raphael to Baldassare Castiglione.

Apart from female beauty, there is also a loving interest in landscape, the countryside, the rivers, trees, birds, cattle and flowers which we see in these paintings. It is a sacred art in the sense that it is inspired, and is a proof of the spiritual exaltation of the Vaishṇava age, No doubt, associative memory plays an important part in the appreciation of art. Liking an art is more a question of understanding. Where, however, the sentiments shown in paintings are universal, they make an immediate appeal even to people who are far away in space and time from the persons who painted them. To an understanding Westerner, not familiar with India or the life of the Hindus, these paintings have a sense of mystery and a quaint charm. It is like reading poetry in a foreign language, in which the unfamiliar words contain a poetry of their own apart from the poetic meaning of them. The very otherworldliness of these paintings has a charm of its own. What enhances their charm is their theme, which is the unwearying tale of human love.

Love which the Hindi poets have extolled is the love of husband and wife. When *parakīya* love is extolled, it is in a spiritual sense, as the love of Rādhā for Kṛishṇa. Otherwise the love norm of Hindu society is that of conjugal fidelity, as of Rāma and Sītā, and Nala and Damayantī. Loyalty is a major force making for unity in life. It gives point and flavour, and above all meaning to a life or culture. Love comes to the Hindus, as to the ancient Greeks, after marriage. When the term lover is used in poetry, it is often synonymous with the 'husband'. The conception of Hindu love is not liaison but married love, a love which is the fruit of long association in the cares and responsibilities of home and children. Even in present-day India, pre-marital chastity is preserved and post-marital fidelity is honoured and widely prevalent, particularly among people not touched by modern education and cinemas.

Love is regarded as profound natural tenderness and solicitude, a serene joy based upon service and interflow between persons. It presumes perfect *entente* between the souls of the man and woman. It is a gift of self to the other in which ego breaks down, and a new being composed of two in one, like *Ardhanārīśvara*, is produced. When the sentiment of love takes possession of body and soul of the persons in love, it results in intense companionship and deep intimacy. Such a love is always sacred and never profane. When it is profane, it is not love, but only lust, a craving for physical satisfaction. One loves not by body alone. It is when body and mind are entirely engrossed in another person, that one loses consciousness of self, and reaches a joyous state of selflessness and absorption in higher self. Thus in its inner rhythm and vibration, it is very close to the ecstasies of divine love. Discussing the theme of love, says Coomaraswamy, "Whatever place is held in the heart of Europe by the love of Dante for his Lady Beatrice, of Paolo for Francesca, of Deirdre for Naoisi, is held in India by the love stories of Rāma and Sītā, of Padmāvatī and Ratan Sen, and the love of Rādhā : in the absolute self-surrender of the human soul in her to the Divine in Kṛishṇa is summed up all love. In this consecration of humanity there is no place for the distinction — always foreign to Indian thought — of sacred and profane. But when in love the finite is brought into presence of the infinite, when the consciousness of inner and outer is destroyed in the ecstasy of union with one beloved, the moment of realisation is expressed in Indian poetry, under the symbol of the speech of Rādhā, the leader of the *gopīs*, with Kṛishṇa, the Divine Cowherd. And Kṛishṇa is the Lord — the ascetic, for whom all earthly beauty is a vain thing, and Rādhā the dancing girl, is the mistress of every art that charms the senses."[4]

Fig. 5. Joy of being together

Thus love which begins in the adoration of physical beauty develops into divine love, and all distinctions of sacred and profane disappear. Ultimately in the union of Rādhā and Kṛishṇa is symbolized the union of the soul with God. When the poet Vidyāpati says, "At any word of dalliance tightly she shuts her eyes, for she has caught a glimpse of the great sea of Love," he describes the union of finite with infinite. Thus love which begins with the adoration of physical beauty, results in the attainment of Absolute Beauty, which is God, Who is also the Trinity of the True, the Good, and the Beautiful.

From adoration of physical beauty the seeker passes on to the love of beauty in Nature. He seeks joy in watching the beauty of mountains, sunrise and sunsets, rain and thunder, and seeks his friends among flowers, birds, and animals, in rocks and water. Thus in the enjoyment of life and Nature he seeks identification of the self with the creative spirit. Thus love extends its circle, becomes infinite, and finds satisfaction in union with Nature. Plato, the Greek philosopher, had a similar experience in his quest for absolute beauty. Thus says Plato, "He who has been instructed thus far in the science of Love, and has been led to see beautiful things in their due order and rank, when he comes toward the end of his discipline, will suddenly catch sight of a wondrous thing, beautiful with the Absolute Beauty; — and this, Socrates, is the aim and end of all those earlier labours — he will see a Beauty Eternal, not growing or decaying, not waxing or waning; nor will it be fair here and foul there, nor depending on time or circumstance or place, as if fair to some and foul to others: nor shall Beauty appear to him in the likeness of a face or hand, nor embodied in any sort of form whatever . . . whether of heaven or of earth; but Beauty absolute, separate, simple, and everlasting; which lending of its virtue to all beautiful things that we see born to decay, itself suffers neither increase nor diminution, nor any other change. When a man proceeding onwards from terrestrial things by the right way of loving, once comes to sight of that Beauty, he is not far from his goal. And this is the right way wherein he should go or be guided in his love; he should begin by loving earthly things for the sake of the absolute loveliness, ascending to that as it were by degrees or steps, from the first to the second, and thence to all fair forms; and from fair forms to fair conduct, and from fair conduct to fair principles, until from fair principles he finally arrives at the ultimate principle of all, and learns what Absolute Beauty is. This life, my dear Socrates, said Diotima, if any life at all is worth living, is the life that a man should live, in the contemplation of Absolute Beauty."[5]

When the seeker in his quest for beauty is in harmony with the spirit of Nature, he sees beauty everywhere and life becomes a pure rapture. The veil which hangs between Nature and consciousness is dense and opaque in the case of insensitive people. For the poet, the mystic and the artist it becomes transparent. Through feeling develops a medium of communication which gives an experience of supreme joy which is incommunicable in language, in the same manner as a dumb person cannot convey the pleasure of eating sugar. Love overflows and gilds the vision and one sees beauty everywhere. There is no more any restlessness and disturbing interplay but only the steady currents of adaptation and sympathy. Truth, Goodness and Beauty are the three attributes of the Supreme Being. Science is the quest after Truth, religion is the quest for Goodness, and art is the quest for Beauty. While science attempts to extract Truth from Nature, art abstracts Beauty. Goodness is in itself a type of Beauty, a harmony of conduct resulting from good actions. Rhythm, harmony, and balance are not only the fundamental principles of the arts of music, painting, architecture, and gardening, but also of religion, which is the art of inner life. In the art of living, which is the highest art, the ideals of Truth, Goodness and Beauty coincide, and science, art and religion are harmonized into a unity of a higher order.

CHAPTER II

BACKGROUND OF THE PAINTINGS

Hindi Love Literature: The *Rasikapriyā* of Keshav Dās

1. CLASSIFICATION OF *NĀYAKAS* AND *NĀYIKĀS*

Most of the paintings reproduced in this book bear excerpts in Devanāgarī script from the poetry of Keshav Dās, Bahādur, Sūr Dās and Bihārī Lāl. Keshav Dās (fl. 1580-1601) was the court poet of Raja Madhukar Shah of Orchha, whose son, Indrajit, gave him a *jāgīr* of twenty-one villages in recognition of his talent. His important works are the *Vigyān Gītā*, the *Rasikapriyā* and the *Kavipriyā*. The *Rasikapriyā* was probably issued in 1591. He wrote the *Kavipriyā* in honour of Rāi Parbīn, the celebrated courtesan of Orchha whom he loved. The Kangra paintings of the *Bārāmāsā* series are inscribed with texts from the *Kavipriyā*, while most of the *Nāyaka-Nāyikā* paintings illustrate texts from the *Rasikapriyā* which seems to have been a favourite with the Kangra painters. Most of the *Nāyaka-Nāyikā* paintings bear inscriptions on the reverse side, but there are some which have no inscriptions, but illustrate various situations described in the chapters of the *Rasikapriyā*. These are the ones which have been given imaginary titles by some authors. The majority of the Kṛishṇa paintings which do not belong to the *Bhāgavata Purāṇa*, the *Gīta Govinda* and the *Satsaiyyā* series are in fact illustrations of the *Rasikapriyā*.

Bihārī Lāl (fl. 1650) was called the 'mine of commentators'. He was the author of seven hundred verses. "Each verse is a perfectly polished jewel; designedly made as artificial as possible and capable of a double meaning." Plate IX illustrates one of Bihārī's *dohās* and there is a whole series on this theme in the collection of the Maharaja of Tehri-Garhwal, out of which some paintings are in the N. C. Mehta collection as well as in the Bhārat Kalā Bhavan, Varanasi. Sūr Dās (fl. 1550) translated the *Bhāgavata Purāṇa* into verse in Vraja Bhāshā. He collected his poems into a compilation entitled the *Sūr Sāgar*. Giving his opinion about the poetry of Sūr Dās, Grierson writes, "Regarding Sūr Dās's place in literature, I can only add that he justly holds a high one. He excelled in all styles. He could, if occasion required, be more obscure than the Sphinx and in the next verse be as clear as a ray of light. Other poets may have equalled him in some particular quality, but he combined the best qualities of all."[6] Plate XX illustrates one of the poems of Sūr Dās, and is a rare example indeed. It is from the collection of the Raja of Lambagraon, and was painted by one of the artists of Maharaja Sansar Chand.

These poets were keen observers of human nature, and their classification of 'Woman' according to age, experience, physical and mental traits, situations, moods and sentiments is remarkable indeed.

The *Rasikapriyā* is a Hindi treatise in verse on rhetoric and literary analysis. Written in a vivid musical style, it has genuine poetic quality. Its theme is love, but it is not the anaemic love of the clasping-of-hands variety of the Northerners of the misty temperate zone, but the full-blooded passion of the sunny monsoon lands. Apart from love, the subject of these poems is religion, a religion which is sincere and passionate. The *nāyaka* and *nāyikā* in Keshav Dās's texts are Kṛishṇa and Rādhā, the ideal lovers, and the situations described show the relationship of the Soul and God.

The poems in the *Rasikapriyā* are miracles of compactness, and in a few words neat little pictures are painted, coloured with the richness and sweetness of a lyrical language. In *dohās*, in a couple of lines, vivid pictures are drawn. On account of their compactness, colourfulness and vividness, the *dohās* of the Hindi poets are particularly suitable as themes for miniature painting.

The earliest illustrations of the *Rasikapriyā* are in Mughal style, and were possibly prepared for presentation to Raja Birbal. Akbar having heard the fame of the hetaira Rāi Parbīn summoned her to his court. Raja Indrajit refused to allow her to go, and thereupon Akbar fined him heavily. This led to a visit by Keshav Dās to the Mughal court to intercede on behalf of his patron, and by display of his poetic talent he won over Birbal, who got the fine remitted. Rāi Parbīn, nevertheless, had to appear before Akbar, and after giving a sample of her learning was allowed to depart. The illustrated *Rasikapriyā*, of which two leaves in the collection of the Metropolitan Museum of Art were described by Coomaraswamy, was dated *circa* A.D. 1600 by him. Soon after the *Rasikapriyā* became a favourite text with the Rajasthani painters, and later on also with the painters in Kangra style. In fact, it is Hindi *Śṛiṅgāra* poetry, the poetry of passion which provides the key to Kangra painting, and most of the Kangra miniatures are really love poems dressed in the form of line and colour.

No great work of art can have vitality unless it is based on experience. The Kangra painters who have so charmingly visualized the poetry of Keshav Dās in line and colour, were themselves keen observers of human beings, and must have had a rich background of experience; otherwise they could not have produced work of such a vital nature. They have shown in the paintings all the stages in the life of a woman, from girlhood to early married life, and middle-aged maturity to old age. The pangs of separation, the unhappiness which jealousy creates, and the joys of reunion are all shown in a vivid manner. These love paintings of the Kangra Valley which portray human feelings in such a remarkable manner were painted by some of the best minds of India, and represent a high achievement of the human spirit.

The structure of the *Rasikapriyā* is as follows: In an opening verse a precise definition of a particular *nāyaka* or *nāyikā*, or an emotional situation is given, followed by one or two illustrations. Besides the speeches of the hero and heroine, the confidantes of the heroine also intervene with their advice, and other words are spoken by the poet himself, who introduces his own name in every verse.

THE *RASAS* (Flavours)

Keshav Dās in the opening chapter of the *Rasikapriyā* describes the nine *rasas* or flavours: *śṛiṅgāra* (the erotic), *hāsya* (the comic), *karuṇa* (the elegiac), *vīra* (the heroic), *raudra* (the terrific), *bhayānaka* (the terrible), *bībhatsa* (the satiric), *śānta* (the quietistic), and *adbhuta* (the sensational).

ŚṚIṄGĀRA

Śṛiṅgāra refers to love as represented in literature. Keshav Dās classifies *śṛiṅgāra* as *saṁyoga* (love in union) and *viyoga* (love in separation). Love in union he sub-classifies as *prachchhanna saṁyoga* (secret love in union), and *prakāśa saṁyoga* (manifested love in union).

Prachchhanna Saṁyoga (Secret Love in Union)

Illustration

"Kṛishṇa and Rādhā in the grove are drinking the honey of each other's beauty; their low murmurings magnify the arts of love, and create desire for forbidden dalliance; Kṛishṇa is beautifully adorned with jewels, making the hearts to beat in great wonder. As he swings his jet black locks, it appears like the Sun holding Saturn in his lap."

Prakāśa Saṁyoga (Manifested Love in Union)

Manifested Love in Union is as follows: "That is Manifested Love in Union, and likewise Manifested Love in Separation," says Keshav Dās, "which everyone comes to realize through (the reflection of) his own picture (in a mirror)."

Illustration

Fig. 6. Manifested love in union (Prakāśa Saṁyoga)

"Once upon a time Kṛishṇa and Rādhā, seated on a *chaukī*, were drenched in the dew of mutual passion, and in delight he beheld in a mirror the radiance of the woman's face; Kṛishṇa was gazing at the

Fig. 7. Manifested love in separation (Prakāśa Viyoga)

scarlet beauty spot between her brows, and moved not his eyes that were filled with the sight, as though it were Rāma gazing upon Sītā (solely), adored by her lord's commands and seated in the fire of sacrifice." (Fig. 6).

Now Keshav Dās defines secret and manifested love in separation:

Prachchhanna Viyoga
(Secret Love in Separation)

"O *sakhī!* there was a time when a mere threat of Kṛishṇa to leave me would pierce my ears like ants. These same ears have heard of his departure but still endure. The eyes, that could not bear his absence for a moment, now see Vraja without him. Now, how can I trust this faithless body which is still shamelessly alive in separation?"

Prakāśa Viyoga
(Manifested Love in Separation)

"O *sakhī!* save me from this tormenting moon and the fragrant breeze. Throw away these flowers, camphor and the sandal-paste; their sight is painful now. To a fish dying without water, milk is of little avail. Do you now understand my condition? The pain of burning can be soothed only by the fire which caused it." (Fig. 7).

CLASSIFICATION OF *NĀYAKAS*

Keshav Dās now gives a definition of *nāyaka*, followed by a classification of *nāyikā*. He defines a *nāyaka* or hero as a man who is young, expert in the art of love, emotional, proud, selfless, generous, handsome, rich and refined in taste and culture. Then he classifies *nāyakas* into four categories: *anukūla* (sincere and devoted), *dakshiṇa* (he who loves all his wives equally), *śaṭha* (unkind and false), and *dhṛishṭa* (shameless).

Anukūla Nāyaka

He who is honest in word, deed and thought, loves his wife and does not care for other women is an *Anukūla Nāyaka* who is the best of men.

Dakshiṇa Nāyaka

He who loves all women equally including his wife or wives is called *Dakshiṇa Nāyaka.*

Śaṭha Nāyaka

He who says sweet words, but is false at heart, and is not afraid of sinning is *Śaṭha Nāyaka.*

Dhṛishṭa Nāyaka

He who does not care for abuse and even beating, and if even seen committing a wrong does not admit his fault is *Dhṛishṭa Nāyaka.*

CLASSIFICATION OF *NĀYIKĀS*

Now follows a classification of *nāyikās* or heroines according to kind into four: *Padminī* (the lotus), *Chitriṇī* (variegated), *Śaṅkhinī* (conch-like), and *Hastinī* (elephant-like).

The *nāyikās* are further classified into *svakīyā* (one's own), *parakīyā* (another's), and *sāmānyā* (anybody's), according to their relationship and response to men. *Svakīyā* is one who loves her own lord; *parakīyā* who loves one who is not her own lord; and *sāmānyā* is one who is impartial. Then follows the classification of *nāyikās* according to their age and experience. The *svakīyā nāyikās* are classified into *mugdhā* (the artless), *madhyā* (adolescent), and *prauḍhā* (mature), who are further sub-classified according to their expertness in the art of love. *Parakīyā nāyikās* are further classified into *ūḍhā* and *anūḍhā*. There are three ways in which the lover may see the beloved, i.e. in person, in a picture, or in a dream. Then follows an account of external indications of emotions and stimuli which awaken erotic feelings. After this the *Eight Nāyikās* are described.

Fig. 8. Detail of Fig. 7

The *sakhīs* or companions of *nāyikās* are also described in detail. They are usually wet-nurses, female servants, wives of barbers, gardeners, betel-sellers or goldsmiths, *sannyāsinīs* or the beggar women. The functions of the *sakhīs* are: giving advice, coaxing, cajoling, helping the lady in her toilet, arranging the meeting of lovers, and carrying messages. The meeting places of lovers are given as the house of a *sakhī*, a vacant or neglected house, fairs and festivals.

A. TYPES OF *NĀYIKĀS*

According to Keshav Dās, women are classified into four types: the Lotus *(Padminī)*, the Variegated *(Chitriṇī)*, the Conch-like *(Śaṅkhinī)* and Elephant-like *(Hastinī)*.

Fig. 9. Adorned with diverse beauties, the chitriṇī is fond of music

i. *Padminī*

Padminī is a beautiful *nāyikā*, emitting the fragrance of a lotus from her body, modest, affectionate and generous, slim, free from anger, and with no great fondness for love-sports. Bashful, intelligent, cheerful, clean and soft-skinned, she loves clean and beautiful clothes. She has a golden complexion.

Illustration

"Shedding flowers from her smile, she is sensitive to tender emotions and knows well the art of love. She is to be preferred to all *Pannagīs*, *Nāgīs*, *Āsurīs* and *Surīs*. All the affection which the people of Vraja bestow on her is in fact too meagre. Thousands of fond desires hover round her like bees. Such indeed is Rādhā, that unique divine *champaka* bud fashioned by the Creator." (Plate I).

ii. *Chitriṇī*

Chitriṇī is adorned with diverse beauties and accomplishments. She is fond of dancing, music and poetry. Tremulous-eyed, steadfast in mind, delighting in love-sports and possessing a sweet-smelling mouth, she is fond of perfumes and her lover's portrait (Fig. 9).

Illustration

One of her friends thus addresses the *Chitriṇī Nāyikā* while she is looking at her husband's portrait:

"The picture speaks not, nor listens when spoken to. Nor does it return the gaze if looked at. It does not sing nor dance nor play the flute. It has none of those pleasing talents to entertain us. It does not relish amorous sports, nor does it embrace you even when seen after long separation. It is unwise to dote on this portrait when it has none of his gifts."

iii. *Śaṅkhinī*

Ill-tempered, and clever, *śaṅkhinī* has a luxuriant growth of hair, likes red garments and pinches hard when excited. She is impatient, shameless and unhesitating.

Illustration

"A camel would never go to a grove where bananas grow. At the sight of such a place an expression of disgust covers his face, as clouds darken the sky. He has no liking for fragrant wreaths of *champaka* blossoms. He shuns the path leading to lotus-beds. He never feeds on sweet smelling clove-vines nor on the tender *lavalī*. If fed on dates and grapes, he dies. He only delights in eating his favourite thorny bushes."[7]

iv. *Hastinī*

Hastinī has thick fingers, a fat face and large feet. Her lower lip and eyebrows are thick and her voice is raucous. Her gait is heavy, her mind infirm. Her tawny hair is of a bitter odour. The hairs on her person are thick, sharp and pointed.

Fig. 10. A fawn ensnared from the forest

Illustration

"It is surprising how that stupid *nāyaka* finds delight in the *nāyikā's* stinking body. Her hair, long and pointed, would pierce holes in his body like thorns. When she opens her mouth to speak, her words jar on the ears. A person who hankers after her is like a bee who leaves fragrant lotus-beds to sit on the temple of a rutting elephant. He is like the king who renounces the earth and his glory, and resorts to evil deeds."

B. CLASSIFICATION OF *NĀYIKĀS* ACCORDING TO AGE

From this Keshav Dās proceeds to another fourfold classification of *nāyikās* according to age: up to sixteen *(bālā)*, from sixteen to thirty *(taruṇī)*, from thirty to fifty-five *(prauḍhā)*, and over fifty-five *(vṛiddhā)*.

C. MAIN CLASSIFICATION OF *NĀYIKĀS*

Keshav Dās's main classification is threefold and distinguishes *nāyikās* as: one's own *(svakīyā)*, another's *(parakīyā)*, and anybody's *(sāmānyā)*.

I. Classification of *Svakīyā Nāyikā*

Svakīyā is devoted to her spouse. Balanced in pleasure and pain, she is true in thought, deed and speech.

According to age and experience *svakīyā* is again divided into three types: the artless *(mugdhā)* (Fig. 12), the adolescent *(madhyā)*, and the mature *(prauḍhā)*.

i. *Mugdhā* or *Navoḍhā*

Mugdhā or *navoḍhā* is again divided into *Navala-vadhū* (the newly wedded), *Navayauvanā* (in fresh youth), *Navala-anaṅgā* (the newly excited), and *Lajjā-prāyā* (the bashful).

Fig. 11. The newly wedded

a. *Navala-vadhū* (The newly wedded)

The old and the learned say that tender in years, this *nāyikā* grows gradually, and her brilliance increases day by day (Fig. 11).

Illustration

"She excels even '*Mohan-mantra*'[8] in the art of bewitching. Who knows how far she will go in learning this art? The growth of her bosom is so rapid that no bodice will be able to check it. The radiance of her eyes increases day by day. O *sakhī*, where will this golden grace end, growing as it is perpetually?"

b. *Navayauvanā* (In fresh youth)

Navayauvanā is the *nāyikā*, who, leaving her childhood behind, has stepped into warm-blooming youth.

Illustration

"At the sight of her husband the *nāyikā's* eyebrows get agitated (Fig. 13). It appears from her figure as if the hips have been robbing the waist for a long time. Her words are few and her eyes downcast. Her gait is no longer girlishly playful. Let her hold her soul in patience, but for a day, for she will soon be united to him — the herald of her youth — who has already entered into her heart and driving her childhood out, has enthroned himself there."

c. *Navala-anaṅgā* (The newly excited)

Navala-anaṅgā is one who plays, speaks, and laughs sportively as children do and wins her husband with her dalliance.

Fig. 12. Mugdhā Nāyikā (The artless)

Illustration

"The young *Navala-anaṅgā* addressed the impassioned bridegroom on the wedding night:

"Oh my darling, desist from excessive haste and eagerness. Pray don't tug at the hem of my cloak. Look, the parrot has gone to sleep in its cage but its mate has not. The lamp burns and sees us furtively — put it out, for you shall see my face even without it. Run up and bolt the door you see in front. My eagerness for what you desire is no less, but first do my bidding and give me solitude." The *nāyikā's* shy suggestion and her dalliance thus enhances his pleasure a hundredfold.

d. *Lajjā-prāyā* (The bashful)

This *nāyikā* takes to erotic play with shyness and timidity and thus enhances the desire of her husband.

Illustration

"He persisted in his protests but I didn't respond. He fell at my feet, but I hid myself in my cloak. He invited me to his bosom with open arms, but I didn't give up my modesty. At last he lifted up my head with his hand pressing against my chin so that our gaze met and I eyed him fondly — Fie at my modesty which could not hold its own and resist his overtures."

Fig. 13. Mugdhā Navayauvanā (In fresh youth)

Now Keshav Dās deals with three other situations regarding *Mugdhā Nāyikās*, the passionate *mugdhā-śayanā*, who is like a sleeping volcano, and can be roused to an extraordinary pitch of passion, the cold and frigid *mugdhā-suratā* who does not respond to love-play, and the *mugdhā's māna*, or obstinacy, and how it can be conquered.

Mugdhā-śayanā

Mugdhā-śayanā Nāyikā is hesitant to set foot on her husband's couch. If persuaded to do so, she creates untold bliss.

Illustration

"The *nāyaka* went down on his knees to entreat the *nāyikā* who at last set her foot on his couch with fear lurking in her heart. Decorating, as it were, the buds strewn over the couch, she somehow went to sleep. Gathering courage, the *nāyaka* touched the *nāyikā's* mouth with his, and was instantly thrown into ecstasies. This roused the *nāyikā* from her slumber who in a single breath released the entire fragrance of her being."

Mugdhā-suratā

Mugdhā-suratā is averse to erotic sports, and prefers a restful night instead. If she is deluded into yielding by force or cunning all pleasure is lost.

Illustration

This verse is a plaint by one of the *mugdhā's* friends which describes the *nāyaka's* guile and trickery which he employed to seduce the *nāyikā* who at the end of the misdeed looks like a crumpled jasmine-garland or an injured lotus-stalk. The verse also expresses the perplexity and remorse of the *nāyaka* after the deed is done.

Fig. 14. One who has stepped into blooming youth

Mugdhā's Māna (Obstinacy)

Though this *nāyikā* is foreign to the sentiment of *māna*, it can be expelled by the exercise of some ingenious threat, such as one we generally practise on credulous, gullible people.

Illustration

"Feigning anger the *mugdhā* sits dumb. Her lord comes and speaks to her but receives no reply. The *nāyikā* silently continues writing with her nails on sand. The *nāyaka's* intelligence comes to his rescue, and looking at his palm with curiosity and earnestness he says : 'The Creator has carved two lines in my palm — one long and the other short. But who can tell which of these represents my age ?' The *nāyikā* could not bear the cruel words and clinging to him breathlessly exclaimed : 'Ah, let me see my love!' "

ii. *Madhyā* (the adolescent)

Madhyā is classified into *Ārūḍhayauvanā*, *Pragalbha-vachanā*, *Prādurbhūta-manobhavā*, and *Surata-vichitrā*.

a. *Ārūḍhayauvanā*

Ārūḍhayauvanā is one who has stepped into blooming youth (Fig. 14).

Illustration

"The *nāyikā's* brow is like the moon, her shapely eyebrows like a bow. Her tremulous, bewitching eyes are like the sharp arrows of Kāmadeva. Her breath has the fragrance of a lotus bud. Her teeth are like pearls and her laughter flashes like lightning. Her belly is shaped like a betel-leaf, her feet like lotuses, and her gait graceful like a swan's. Such a cow-girl resembling a goddess with a golden complexion have I seen, O Gopāl!"

b. *Pragalbha-vachanā*

Pragalbha-vachanā is one who cleverly scolds her husband with her words and thus irritates him.

Illustration

The *nāyikā* says sarcastically to the unfaithful *nāyaka:*

"You are indeed very magnanimous, and noble are your ways. How chaste were those eyes whose colour still lingers in yours! I know all that comes into your mind, and what those greedy sirens desire of you. Wherever you go, groves and gardens grow, and you are a creator of happiness and giver of delight to your paramours. But desist from stirring out today. You have been deluded by false friends, and I am bent upon saving you from them."

c. *Prādurbhūta-manobhavā*

Prādurbhūta-manobhavā is one who is as if ornamented by the lore of Kāmadeva which pervades her body and mind.

Illustration

"Today I saw the daughter of a milkman — a rare gem among cow-girls. Seeing the comeliness of her radiant face, all other beautiful objects sink into nothingness, and one looks at her as if spellbound. In return for a single upward movement of her eyes, I would fain give away the entire wealth of the three worlds. The God of Love has well selected Kṛishṇa — the source of erotic sciences — to be her lord."

d. *Surata-vichitrā*

The amorous nature of this *nāyikā* comprises strange elements, and presents formidable difficulties for poets to describe it. Yet it is ever pleasing.

Illustration

The *nāyikā* thus relates her experiences to her confidante:

"Our delight is enhanced by soft subdued laughter and dalliance. Fond looks and whispers are so pleasing. All the fourteen types of *bahī-rati* and *antara-rati* are practised by us. And then comes *viparīta-rati* which destroys all charm of modesty, so that ornaments get displaced and tresses become dishevelled. Necklaces snap and all adornments vanish. Such, indeed, is genuine passion which proclaims itself aloud and hearing which birds themselves begin to warble."

Fig. 15. The timid bride

Now Keshav Dās gives a classification of *bahī-rati* or preliminaries of love-play, and of *antara-rati* or union. According to him there are seven types each of *bahī-rati* and *antara-rati.*

Bahī-rati (Preliminaries of love-play)

Embracing, kissing, gentle fondling, pressing, making marks by nails and teeth and sucking of lips are known as seven preliminaries of love making.

Antara-rati (Postures in union)

Seven intimate postures in union are: standing, lateral, face-to-face, face-to-back, facing downward, facing upward, and lying on the back.

The passion for classification, which the Hindi poets and rhetoricians have, is truly remarkable. Now Keshav Dās gives a classification of the toilet of a fashionable woman of his age. He classifies the toilet and make-up of a young lady into sixteen types.

Solā Śṛiṅgāra (Sixteen types of adornments)

Bathing, putting on clean and beautiful clothes, applying *mahāvar* (red lac dye) to the feet, dressing hair, using five *aṅgarāgas* (vermilion on the parting of the hair, painting sandal-paste mark on the forehead, a mole on the cheek, saffron on the body, and *henna* on the palms), wearing ornaments and flowers, cleaning teeth and chewing betel and cardamom, rubbing *missi* (a fragrant paste) on the teeth, reddening the lips, and painting eye-lashes with collyrium, are the sixteen adornments for a woman. "Oh Rādhā, adorn your person with these *śṛiṅgāras*, smile softly, talk sweetly, walk gently, and look charming. And with all these live a chaste married life."

ANOTHER CLASSIFICATION OF *MADHYĀ* (THE ADOLESCENT)

Keshav Dās now gives another threefold classification of *madhyā* according to the manner in which she addresses her husband.

Madhyā is of three types: *Dhīrā*, *Adhīrā* and *Dhīrādhīrā*. *Dhīrā* speaks in an oblique manner, *adhīrā* speaks harsh words and *dhīrādhīrā* scolds her husband.

a. *Dhīrā* (The firm)

Dhīrā — the *nāyikā* is trembling with anger, but out of modesty she conceals her emotion from the *sakhī*, and attributes her trembling to other reasons.

"*Sakhī*, you told me that my lord's face resembled a lotus, but I discover that it is like the moon, for look! as he proceeded to enter my heart, my bosom began to shiver violently, and it appeared as if it were affected by some unknown chill. My eye-lotuses stood as if carved in stone or shaped in a mould."

b. *Adhīrā* (The fickle)

Nāyikā, scoldingly to *nāyaka:*

"Your body is like your father's (i.e. worn out and lean with age), your valour is like Balavīra's (who got most of his strength from intoxicants), your face resembles your sister's (according to some, an inauspicious thing). Your conduct is barren like a desert, devoid as it is of all goodness. Your mind is as infirm as the winds. Your lustre is as unstrained as stagnant water. Like the glowing skies you distribute your radiance in every home."

c. *Dhīrādhīrā*

Nāyikā to unfaithful *nāyaka:*

"You are noble, and noble must have been your *gurus*. But it is queer that you are exhibiting such an emotion for another woman. What did you get as reward in exchange for your jewel of a heart which you gave away to her?

"Is it now possible for you to mingle your gaze with mine?

"Don't blame me for I am only depending on hearsay, and on what you have been telling my friends."

iii. *Prauḍhā* (The mature)

Prauḍhā is classified into *Samasta-rasa-kovidā*, *Vichitra-vibhramā*, *Ākrāmitā*, and *Labdhā-pati.*

a. *Samasta-rasa-kovidā*

The *nāyikā*, who provides to her lover whatever pleasure he seeks in her, is called *samasta-rasa-kovidā prauḍhā*, or expert in the art of love.

Illustration

"O Gopāl, I saw a cow-girl of peerless beauty comparable only to gold, who shone brilliantly in her dress. Was she the personification of Rati or was she a flash of lightning disguised as a woman? It is hard to determine whether she was some divine nymph who fled from the domain of her tribe, or some novel grace sent by Sarasvatī. I believe, however, that she must have been the incarnate accomplishment of the means of all pleasure, and the best specimen of Kāmadeva's craftsmanship."

b. *Vichitra-vibhramā*

Vichitra-vibhramā is she whose best messenger is her exquisite charm which wins her lover.

Illustration

"Her slow and graceful gait feeds the creeping delight of his heart. Her tremulous eyebrows and soft silken laughter and perfumed limbs have clasped him firmly. The gaze from the corners of her eyes has 'fatally' wounded Kṛishṇa. Her looks are the arrows of Kāmadeva, and the *nāyaka*, being unaware of that, fell a prey to them, like the ignorant bee, which ardently sucking honey from the flower is caught at nightfall when the petals close upon her."

c. *Ākrāmitā*

Ākrāmitā is one who by means of all the devices of speech, thought, and deed endeavours to win her lover and succeeds.

Fig. 16. Parakīyā Nāyikā (One who loves a person other than her lord)

Sakhī to nāyikā:

"For your sake the poor lad sings, dances, and plays on his flute and adorns himself. He doesn't even think of any other damsel. Still he doesn't succeed in capturing your heart. You should thank your stars that he is so devoted to you. Do you now long for the simple-hearted boy to come and kiss your feet?"

d. *Labdhā-pati*

Labdhā-pati is one whose authority is supreme, and the entire family of her husband listens to her respectfully and praises her.

Illustration

"Gopāl, there sits today the comely daughter of Vṛishabhānu. This charming bride of yours was created by Kāmadeva in the manner Brahmā created Sarasvatī. Having seen her, who can think of another? Beauty — having adorned herself — has today approached the personification of *Śṛiṅgāra.*"

Prauḍhā-dhīrā

Prauḍhā-dhīrā is one who with all her obedience does service but occasionally shows disregard and hides herself.

Illustration

Seeing Kṛishṇa approach her, she gets up to receive him and offers him a good seat. She herself washes his feet and brings a new vessel to offer him a drink. She places delicious food before him and takes up the fan. At this he catches her arm and beseeches her to give him a smile first, but she suddenly turns her face and stands quietly (Plate IV).

Prauḍhā-dhīrā-ākṛitiguptā

Sakhī to nāyikā:

"Why do you lift your gaze only when looked at, laugh only when tickled, speak only when spoken to; for otherwise you are always cold and unresponsive? And why do you weep when he approaches you with his protestations of love and offers you his affectionate lap? You don't even eat anything unless compelled to: it appears as if it were your first day in the house of your in-laws. Who taught you this novel lesson to win Mohan? Mind your welfare and listen to what is beneficial and what will make you comfortable. Your conduct has false propriety, and does not become your natural self. You insult your dear ones when they honour you.

"Now look, don't try to suppress your laughter. Let it gently flow!"

Prauḍhā-adhīrā

Prauḍhā-adhīrā is one who longs to meet her husband, but speaks dry words though she is herself as sweet as sugarcane juice. Holding him guilty she honours him not, though he honours her.

The *nāyikā*, suspicious of the *nāyaka's* fidelity, scolds him thus:

"Your mind is polluted with dirt and sin. Give up your sweet utterances and desist from laughing. Don't trouble me any more with your nice words and amorous play at night — I have had enough of them all."

Seeing the *nāyaka's* eyes dimmed with passion, she says:

"Look, your dull eyes are preparing to close — only to gleam in other women's presence. You are still the same faithless rake that you were yesterday, although you took a thousand oaths then."

II. Classification of *Parakīyā Nāyikās*

Parakīyās are of two types — *ūḍhā* and *anūḍhā*. They are perplexing types for both the wise and the foolish.

A *parakīyā* is one who is fond of being the sweetheart of celebrities. *Ūḍhā* is married and *anūḍhā* is unmarried. Their respective traits are thus described by the poet:

Ūḍhā

"Decorating the assembly of her friends with her presence, she is as if dwelling in their eyes. When questioned about them she wilfully speaks false philosophic words about the weakness of flesh, the guilt of her husband and the woes of separation, but laughs in her sleeve. Why, nobody even noticed her when suddenly catching sight of him she slipped away!"

Anūḍhā

On the day Rādhā's father promised her hand to Hari, the blessed Rādhā was sitting in the midst of the ladies of Vraja absorbed in a game of *chaupāḍ*. Suddenly hearing the voice of Hari, who had come there on a false pretext, she was seized by a strong emotion and her heart throbbed, and without anybody noticing her, she flung the arrow of her glance in the direction from which the voice came.

Anūḍhā betrays her secrets to none, while *ūḍhā* confides in her *sakhīs*.

Ūḍhā relates to her friend her experiences in the city of her lord:

"The womenfolk slandered me and smiled at me and not a soul spared me. I looked stupidly on all sides with eyes tremulous as a *chakorī's*; and with everybody's finger pointing at me, I was made as if the moon of the second lunar night."[9]

There is an amusing picture from Guler in which a *parakīyā nāyikā* of *ūḍhā* variety is shown. A paṇḍit is reading a *Purāṇa* to an audience of villagers. The elders are seated on one side, and women opposite. Rādhā is sitting in front of the paṇḍit and the scarf of her husband Ayana is tied to her *dupaṭṭā* showing that they are husband and wife. Kṛishṇa comes and joins the assembly. On seeing Kṛishṇa, Rādhā forgets all about her marital ties, and veiling her face from her husband glances furtively at Kṛishṇa[10](Fig. 16).

CHAPTER III

THE MOODS OF LOVERS AND THEIR MEETING PLACES

Dampatī Cheshṭā Varṇana

In Chapter V of the *Rasikapriyā*, Keshav Dās describes the moods of lovers and the places and situations in which they meet. How the *nāyaka* and the *nāyikā* behave when they are in love, and how they reveal their desire, though outwardly concealing it, is thus described by Keshav Dās:

Fig. 17. Yearnings of love

SECRET DESIRE OF RĀDHĀ
Rādhā's *Cheshṭā (Prachchhanna)*

Sometimes she scratches the ear, sometimes yawns and stretches the limbs (Figs. 17 and 18). She also laughs and talks to her *sakhī*, thus attracting the attention of her lover and displaying her graces. By these clever artifices she expresses her love to him.

SECRET DESIRE OF KṚISHṆA
Kṛishṇa's *Cheshṭā (Prakāśa)*

"Absent-mindedly you stand before the mirror tidying your turban. Who is she in whose love you are lost so entirely and at whose feet you want to throw yourself? Sometimes you snap your fingers, and sometimes you scratch your ear. Why are you yawning and stretching your limbs as if in fever? Who is she for whom you are giving your pearl necklace to me, and why are you singing incoherently? Oh Kṛishṇa, tell me what is wrong with you today?"

Keshav Dās describes the places and situations in which lovers meet.

The house of a female servant, friend, and foster-mother, an empty house, and the forest are the places where the first meetings of lovers are arranged. They also meet in a situation of fear, on an excuse of an invitation to meals, or sickness, or at a festival.

MEETING AT A FEMALE SERVANT'S HOUSE

(Dāsī Ghar Milan)

Disguised as a girl, Kṛishṇa fearlessly joined the Vraja maidens in their sports at night. Cleverly he managed to play with Rādhā, who gleamed like lightning, looked like a creeper of love or a love-noose, and threw his arms around her back. Running around and hiding with her in the game of hide-and-seek, he satisfied his heart's desire and played innumerable tricks of love. Thus in the courtyard of the *Dāsī's* house did Kṛishṇa convert the game of hide-and-seek into the game of love.

MEETING AT THE HOUSE OF A CONFIDANTE

(Sahelī Ghar Milan)

Sakhī says to Kṛishṇa :

"O Kṛishṇa, keep her as pupils of your eyes, or as you hold your flute between the lips, or your garland of wild flowers between your arms, or the sandal-paste painted on your arms. Keep close, as you keep your garland of wild flowers, this sweet-voiced girl, whom I have somehow led to this house. Keep in your heart this maiden, who resembles a goddess; and take delight from the fragrance of her *champaka*-like limbs."

Fig. 18. Love longings

MEETING AT A FOSTER-MOTHER'S HOUSE

(Dhāi Ghar Milan)

The cow-boys and cow-girls played and laughed and told each other stories and riddles in the foster-mother's house till late in the night, and the light of the sinking moon had grown dim. Overpowered by sleep, they gradually proceeded homewards. Seeing dark clouds rising on all sides in the sky, Kṛishṇa also rose to depart, when the kind foster-mother thus spoke: "Where will you go, dear child, in the darkness at the dead of night? Go and sleep, sharing half of Rādhā's bed."

MEETING IN AN EMPTY HOUSE

(Śūnya Ghar Milan)

Rādhā was alone in a picture gallery. Looking at a picture, she felt happy and began to dance. The jingle of her anklets, the rhythmical movements of her feet, and her singing were delightful. At that moment Kṛishṇa appeared, and at the sight of him Rādhā's appearance became indescribable. Struggling between modesty and passion, her lotus-like eyes had the semblance of a water-laden cloud.

MEETING ON A JOURNEY AT NIGHT

(Niśā Milan)

Once a group of cow-boys and cow-girls went to Gokula. Night fell as they were returning, and clouds covered the sky. It was so dark that they could hardly see each other. On such a night, "Dear *sakhī*, Kṛishṇa made the most of it; he did with freedom what he chose, and relieved himself of the pain of separation."

MEETING IN A SITUATION OF FEAR

(Atibhaya Milan)

The house of Vṛishabhānu, Rādhā's father, caught fire. People of Vraja ran to the scene and climbed on the walls all round. There was noise and confusion everywhere. Taking advantage of such a situation, Kṛishṇa went into the house, put the *mainā* and the parrot out, and roused the women of the household who rushed out. Rādhā he roused last of all, and kissed her eyes, chin and cheeks. Her body resembling a garland of *champaka* clung to his bosom (Fig. 21).

MEETING AT A FESTIVAL

(Utsava Milan)

To celebrate the birthday of Balarāma, the beauties of Vraja, with limbs of gold, gathered in the house of Nanda to keep vigil for the night. There was such a crowd that not a corner of the house was left unoccupied. The women sang and danced and played on musical instruments, thus producing a stream of delight.

In this situation, Rādhā slept in the bed of Kṛishṇa: he came and laid himself there, as if it was the night of his honeymoon.

Fig. 19. Rādhā's manifested desire

MEETING ON AN EXCUSE OF ILLNESS

(Vyādhi miss Milan)

Having diagnosed the cause of the disease, offerings of gifts were made to placate the evil stars. Medicines were given but the disease showed no sign of abatement. Offerings to the fire were made according to command of the scriptures, but the pain was not cured.

"Hurry up, O Kṛishṇa! You have been called, the condition of Rādhā is precarious. The pain of which you cured her last time has recurred."

MEETING ON THE PRETEXT OF AN INVITATION

(Nimantraṇa miss Milan)

Yaśodā invited Rādhā to supper at her house. Having adorned her face, Yaśodā took her to the dining parlour. After the meals, chewing a betel, Rādhā went upstairs to see the house and encountered Kṛishṇa. Seeing the handsome Kṛishṇa, she ran back, but he, taking courage, caught her by her snake-like tress. Taking her into his lap, he caressed her and did what he liked. And, then, having taken off her nose-ring, he rubbed her face with saffron to conceal the marks of his passionate love and let her go.

Fig. 20. Lovers in a lily pool

MEETING IN THE FOREST

(Vana Vihāra Milan)

Says Kṛishṇa to a *gopī* whom he met in the forest:

"You had promised yesterday to give me curds. Give them to me now.

Spread your garment and then your waist-band to fill them with curds but let me go.

I will allow you to go, if you persuade Rādhā to discard her shyness."

"Mind your words, lest someone else should hear them.
Don't you know whose daughter she is?

I know she is Vṛishabhānu's daughter;
but I know not whom you serve."

MEETING AT WATER SPORTS

(Jala Vihāra Milan)

Illustration 1

Rādhā and Kṛishṇa stand on the bank of Mānasarovara, clasping each other's hands. Kṛishṇa is wearing a turban, Rādhā is wearing pearls, and flower garlands are adorning both. They are draped in white, and their limbs are painted with sandal-paste. It appears as if Vishṇu, accompanied by Lakshmī, has emerged from the ocean of milk (Fig. 20).

Illustration 2

Every day in the summer months, cow-boys and cow-girls play in the water of the Yamunā. Cow-girls are on one side of the river, and Kṛishṇa with a crowd of cow-boys is on the other. The two groups of lovers dive into the water like fish, and having met each other under water, they emerge on their own side of the river. In this manner, they satisfy their longings with craft, apparently remaining away from each other.

Fig. 21. Lovers meeting in a situation of fear

CHAPTER IV

EXTERNAL INDICATIONS OF EMOTIONS OF LOVE

Hāva

The manifestation of a mental state through the face, eyes and speech is said to be *bhāva*. *Bhāvas* are of five types: *vibhāva*, *anubhāva*, *sthāyī*, *sāttvika* and *vyabhichārī*. A stimulus which awakens the erotic flavour is called an excitant *(vibhāva)*. Excitants are of two kinds, essential *(ālaṁbana)*, which sustain love, and *uddīpana* which cause excitement. The flavour *(rasa)* is absolutely dependent on an essential excitant which is material and necessary to it. The hero or the heroine is the essential or the material ingredient of the flavour, without which the flavour cannot be created. The other excitants are those which enhance the flavour: *sakhīs*, moonlight, clouds, lightning, rainbow, flowers, perfume, drinks, ornaments, beautiful clothes, a decorated bed, colours, dance, music, painting, the *koel's* song, and the humming of bees. *Uddīpana* is caused by looking at one's beloved, conversing with her, embracing, kissing, touching and pressing her, and by wounding her body with teeth and nails. The gesture or movement that gives rise to a flavour is called an ensuant *(anubhāva)*. Of these, the swaying of the body, the motion of the eyebrows, and side-glances are important.

An underlying emotion or underlying sentiment *(sthāyī bhāva)* is the ultimate ground-basis of a poetic work, and is the permanent condition, which, running through the other conditions like the thread of a garland, is not overpowered by them but only reinforced. The underlying emotions are of eight kinds, e.g. love or desire *(rati)*, mirth *(hāsa)*, sorrow *(śoka)*, anger *(krodha)*, magnanimity *(utsāha)*, fear *(bhaya)*, dispraise *(nindā)*, and surprise *(vismaya)*. The underlying emotions produce the corresponding flavours or psychic conditions in the reader.

Sāttvika bhāvas are the eight involuntary expressions of emotions, viz. stupor, trembling, speechlessness, pallor, tearfulness, perspiration, thrill and fainting.

Vyabhichārī bhāva is an accessory emotion that goes along with any one of the underlying emotions *(sthāyī bhāva)*, which form the foundations of nine flavours. These accessory emotions are thirty-three in number, viz. self-disparagement *(nirveda)*, apprehension or anticipation of evil *(śaṅkā)*, arrogance *(garva)*, painful reflection *(chintā)*, distraction *(moha)*, despondency *(vishāda)*, depression *(dainya)*, envy *(asūyā)*, death *(mṛityu)*, intoxication *(mada)*, indolence *(ālasya)*, weariness *(śrama)*, derangement *(unmāda)*, dissembling *(ākṛiti-*

gopana), unsteadiness *(chapalatā)*, dementedness *(apasmāra)*, alarm *(bhaya)*, debility *(glāni)*, shame *(vrīḍā)*, stupor *(jaḍatā)*, joy *(harsha)*, equanimity *(dhṛti)*, resolve *(mati)*, flurry *(āvega)*, longing *(utkaṇṭhā)*, drowsiness *(nidrā)*, dreaming *(svapna)*, awaking *(bodha)*, sternness *(ugratā)*, impatience of opposition *(amarsha)*, debate *(vitarka)*, sickness *(vyādhi)* and recollection *(smṛti)*.

EXTERNAL INDICATIONS OF LOVE *(HĀVA)*

The 'external indications of emotion' in a hero and a heroine occasioned by love in union are called *hāva*, and are of thirteen kinds. *Līlā-hāva* is the enjoyment of amorous caresses by the lovers. In *vilāsa-hāva*, 'flutter of delight', the eyes of the heroine shine with happiness. When the hero's charm is displayed through his smart dress and decorations, it is called *lalita-hāva*, or 'voluptuous gracefulness'. The wearing of simple clothes and a few ornaments by a woman confident of her personal charm is considered to be an indication of love, and is called *vichchhiti-hāva*. Flustered at the arrival of her lover, the heroine wears her ornaments at the wrong places and this is called *vibhrama-hāva*. Sometimes the emotions of anger, joy, desire and fear are strangely mixed, and the resulting 'hysterical delight' is called *kilakiñchita-hāva*. Sometimes the heroine yawns, or stretches her limbs on hearing her loved one talked of in praise. These mute involuntary expressions of affection are called *moṭṭāyita-hāva*. When the heroine pretends to be indifferent to the arrival of her lover, making a show of anger and uttering unpleasant words though her heart is full of love, the display of emotion is called *bibboka-hāva*. When the heroine under the influence of love forgets her modesty, her wantonness is called *helā-hāva*. When a hero

Fig. 22. Rādhā and Kṛishṇa exchange clothes

communicates his feelings to the heroine by signs or by a riddle, it is called *bodha-hāva* or *bodhaka-hāva*, e.g. a lover presents a withered lotus to the lady to indicate the condition of his heart. Affected repulse of endearments, where the heroine, though enraptured by endearments, displays the reverse is called *kuṭṭamita-hāva*. *Mada-hāva* is arrogance arising from love. When the heroine or hero is not able to speak on account of bashfulness, it is called *vikṛita-hāva*. The love of Kṛishṇa and Rādhā produces the various forms of *hāva*; their sports, dalliance, sweet intoxication and amorous playfulness manifest *kilakiñchita*, *moṭṭāyita*, *kuṭṭamita*, and *bodha*.

Now Keshav Dās describes thirteen kinds of *hāva* which the love of Rādhā and Kṛishṇa produces. There are a whole series of paintings on the *hāvas* in Rajasthani art and also some in Kangra art.

Fig. 23. Rādhā's Līlā-hāva (Rādhā puts on Kṛishṇa's clothes)

WANTONNESS *(HELĀ-HĀVA)*

Love in its ripeness makes them forget bashfulness as well as the people around; Kṛishṇa and Rādhā are indeed bewitching in this *Helā*.

Rādhā's *Helā-hāva*

Attracting him with her looks, then capturing him by means of the wondrous noose of her eyebrows, she met him in solitude in the moonlit night, with a smile on her face and fragrance around her. She then enslaved him by making him drink the wine of her lips. Thus, with ease, the daughter of Vṛishabhānu won Hari in the forest (Plate V).

Kṛishṇa's *Helā-hāva*

Rādhā's heart overflowed with delight to see the *Rāsa-līlā* ground in bloom in the forest, where she was drawn by the notes of Kṛishṇa's flute. Kissing her with ardour and pressing her in his arms, the artful Kṛishṇa won the heart of Vṛishabhānu's daughter, as if in sport.

SPORT (*LĪLĀ-HĀVA*)

When the lovers imitate each other's manners, *Līlā-hāva* is created (Figs. 22 and 23).

Rādhā's *Līlā-hāva*

Rādhā imitates and learns Kṛishṇa's ways of falling at her feet unmindful of insults, his offering the betel-leaf and eating it himself with dalliance, his confused glance wandering on all sides, his being startled at the sound of the rustling of dry leaves, and his going from one bower to another with closed eyes.

Fig. 24. Kṛishṇa's voluptuous gracefulness

Kṛishṇa's *Līlā-hāva*

Kṛishṇa imitates Rādhā peeping from the attic window and running to the roof-top to catch a glance, her ridiculing the conduct of the cow-boys, her prayers in meditation of Kṛishṇa, her engrossment in the joy of looking at the portrait of her lover and hugging it, her going from the house to the courtyard and from the courtyard back to the house, and thus spending the whole day.

Exchange of clothes is another mode of lovers' *Līlā-hāva*. Rādhā is wearing Kṛishṇa's crown of peacock feathers and garland of white flowers, while Kṛishṇa is wearing a *ghāghrā* and is draped in *dupaṭṭā* (Fig. 22). In another painting the lovers are sitting in dalliance on a carpet of leaves, and Kṛishṇa has placed his garland on Rādhā's neck and his crown on her head (Fig. 23).

VOLUPTUOUS GRACEFULNESS (*LALITA-HĀVA*)

Speech, laughter, winsome looks and gait are the creators of *Lalita-hāva*.

Rādhā's *Lalita-hāva*

Going with her Sarasvatī-like *sakhī*, the tender and pure-hearted Rādhā appears like Lakshmī carrying a beautiful lotus. The sound of her ringing anklets is throwing the terrified swans off their feet. The load of her heavy tresses, her heavy hips and her hesitation are bending her tender waist. Her soft words, low laughter, amorous glances and ambling gait have won the heart of young Kṛishṇa.

Kṛishṇa's *Lalita-hāva*

"The fluttering hem of his yellow garment resembles the lightning; the shining crown of peacock feather is enhancing his beauty like the rainbow. He sings in low tones and plays upon the flute. His approach creates the illusion of the advent of clouds, which makes the peacocks dance. Look, *sakhī*, the fire of *chātaka's* heart is being quenched, as handsome Kṛishṇa, dark as the cloud, wearing cloud-like garments, emerges from the deep forest into Vraja."

Fig. 25. Kṛishṇa's Lalita-hāva

ARROGANCE *(MADA-HĀVA)*

Arrogance arising from love is *Mada-hāva*.

Rādhā's *Mada-hāva*

"Revelling in her dalliance the proud Rādhā had drunk heavily the wine of her beauty and pride, when young Kṛishṇa, fairer than Kāmadeva, came to propitiate her. The poor lad took oath after oath, laughed, and fell at her feet till his heart sank in dejection. Then, suddenly, dark clouds arose, seeing which Rādhā leapt like lightning to the bosom of Kṛishṇa." (Fig. 26).

Kṛishṇa's *Mada-hāva*

'No charming woman can win 'him now. He knows the fickleness of lightning, he listens not to the protestations of Rati's love; he knows too the waning lustre of the digit of the moon. Leave alone others, even the fair Lakshmī cannot propitiate him, maddened as he is by his love for Rādhā who alone is enthroned in his heart."

FLUSTER *(VIBHRAMA-HĀVA)*

Where, through hurry arising from delight, the beloved one wears ornaments in the wrong way, and when the sight of the lover delights the body and the mind, *Vibhrama-hāva* is said to be created.

Rādhā's *Vibhrama-hāva*

Rādhā on hearing the news of the arrival of Kṛishṇa put the necklace round her waist, and the jingling girdle round her neck. She put the anklets on her wrists and the bracelets on her feet. She forgot to cover her bodice with her mantle, painted her beautiful cheeks with collyrium and her eyes with red foot-paint. Thus bedecking herself, Rādhā hastened to have a glimpse of Kṛishṇa, the ornament of Vraja.

Kṛishṇa's *Vibhrama-hāva*

Kṛishṇa, whose body is covered with sandal-paste, is playing. The sight of Rādhā infatuates his mind, and, forgetful of the betel-leaf which has fallen from his hand, he starts chewing the lotus-leaf which he is holding in the other hand. Seeing this, the *gopīs* burst into laughter. Out of bashfulness he has now concealed the beauty of his eyelashes by closing his eyes.

Fig. 26. On hearing the peal of thunder the lady leapt like lightning to the bosom of her lover

BASHFULNESS *(VIKṚITA-HĀVA)*

At the time of meeting, modesty holds back the tongue and thus creates *Vikṛita-hāva.*

Rādhā's *Vikṛita-hāva*

"You are not giving up bashfulness, and my words of advice irritate you; but a time will come when you will burn your bashfulness in the heat of your love. Having plunged into the ocean of love how long will you depend on the help of others? It is the great desire of all your *sakhīs* that you may greet your lover smilingly. How long will you thus remain passive like a picture?"

Kṛishṇa's *Vikṛita-hāva*

Rādhā accused Kṛishṇa of fickleness, reprimanded him and hit him with a lotus, her love for him drying up with anger. Cooling down, she gave him wise advice which he accepted with joy. She presented him with perfumed gifts which he pressed to his heart. Despite all this, Kṛishṇa did not say anything, nor did he raise his head.

FLUTTER OF DELIGHT
(VILĀSA-HĀVA)

When in play, speech, laughter, looks and deportment, reserve is discarded, a flutter of delight is created (Fig. 27).

Rādhā's *Vilāsa-hāva*

"O *sakhī*, the radiant *tilaka* on your forehead delights him; the constant dalliance of your eyebrows produces different impulses in his mind; your eyes expressive of thought and hesitation are tremulous, and the glitter of your teeth bewilders his mind. Your soft laughter and sweet breath have effortlessly enslaved the heart of Kṛishṇa. Indeed your charming face has taken a hundred vows to capture the body and heart of Kṛishṇa."

Fig. 27. Flutter of delight

Kṛishṇa's *Vilāsa-hāva*

"Those who have not seen your beautiful eyes are longing to see them. They, who have seen them once, do not wish to see anything else. These eyes are dear as life to mortals, gods, *nāgas*, and to *pañchakanyā*, Ahalyā, Tārā, Kuntī, Mandodarī and Draupadī. They dwell in the hearts of the most devout wives. All your limbs too are infinitely beautiful, whose parallel Brahmā has not been able

Fig. 28. Lady's message of love

to create. O Kṛishṇa, your eyes can shatter the pride of beauty, the vanity of Kāmadeva, and the vows of steadfast women."

HYSTERICAL DELIGHT *(KILAKIÑCHITA-HĀVA)*

When emotions of desire, pride, anger, joy and alarm are aroused simultaneously, *Kilakiñchita-hāva* is manifested.

Rādhā's *Kilakiñchita-hāva*

"Seeing whom do you laugh and exult? And seeing whom do you frown in anger? Why do you sometimes become forgetful of your modesty, and sometimes hide your face with the hem of your garment? For whose welfare are you offering prayers? Your queer ways make me sick. You were never like this before. May you not lose your wits!" (Fig. 30).

Kṛishṇa's *Kilakiñchita-hāva*

"Which is the damsel in Gokula who has diverted your eyes from all others exclusively towards her? Like a *khañjana* bird sporting in the creepers, your eyes are playful. But why are you irritated when spoken to, and desirous when left alone? Why do you sometimes lurk timidly and sometimes look spirited? What love potion have you taken that all beauty other than that of the beloved is distasteful to you like poison?"

AFFECTATION OF INDIFFERENCE *(BIBBOKA-HĀVA)*

When the pride of beauty and love causes feigned insult and respect is not shown to the beloved on his arrival, but on the contrary anger is displayed, *Bibboka-hāva* becomes manifest.

Rādhā's *Bibboka-hāva*

Aware of Kṛishṇa's approach, Rādhā lay down feigning sleep. Not wanting to rouse her, Kṛishṇa sat silently by her side. Taking courage, he touched her leg which caused the hair of her body to stand up on end. When he proceeded to unlace the cord of her *ghāghrā* Rādhā got up startled, and—though recognizing him—upbraided him in annoyance like this: "O ill-bred cow-boy, you graze the cows the whole day, how dare you approach another woman's bed at night?"

Kṛishṇa's *Bibboka-hāva*

Once Kṛishṇa said these words to a *gopī* out of fun: "Given up by your father, how can you nurse feelings of love for me?"

This brought a flood of tears into the eyes of the *gopī*. Kṛishṇa, greatly touched, embraced her, but leaning against him, she sobbed till midnight.

SIMPLICITY IN DRESS *(VICHCHHITI-HĀVA)*

When the beauty of ornaments is disregarded, *Vichchhiti-hāva* is aroused.

Rādhā's *Vichchhiti-hāva*

"These ornaments which you like are in fact useless as compared with the grace and beauty of your person. Kṛishṇa's eyes thirst for the loveliness of your limbs, which being your real ornaments, you can never put off. Perfumes spread their sweetness all round, but can the natural fragrance of a perfume be separated from it? Ornaments cannot decorate you, O Rādhā, it is you who decorate them."

Kṛishṇa's *Vichchhiti-hāva*

"You have refused to accept betel-leaf and to decorate your turban. You have changed your lovely clothes, and have thrown away your pearl necklace and the garland of wild flowers. You have disfigured the sandal paint on your limbs; and your gaze you have withdrawn from the world around. But who can destroy the natural majesty and fragrance of your limbs?"

MUTE INVOLUNTARY EXPRESSION OF AFFECTION (*MOṬṬĀYITA-HĀVA*)

When unhesitant dalliance and sportive love, producing *Sāttvika-bhāva*, are restrained by wisdom's might, *Moṭṭāyita-hāva* becomes manifest.

Rādhā's *Moṭṭāyita-hāva*

Wearing a beautiful robe, Kṛishṇa is sporting, where Rādhā, prettier than Rati, sits. Suddenly noticing on the back of Kṛishṇa the red marks of *sindūra* (which had been imprinted from her bosom by an embrace on an earlier occasion), Rādhā, on account of the nearness of her mother, concealed her emotion by putting powdered camphor into her eyes, smelling a lotus, and wrapping her mantle around her body. (The emotions concealed are tearfulness by the use of camphor, tremulousness by smelling a lotus, and horripilation and pallor by wearing a mantle.)

Fig. 29. Kṛishṇa's message of love

Kṛishṇa's *Moṭṭāyita-hāva*

Invited to Vṛishabhānu's house, Kṛishṇa, Balavīra and many other cow-boys were sitting

Fig. 30. Rādhā's hysterical delight

together after lunch with the host; and Kṛishṇa was making betel-leaves and eating them. With the sudden appearance of Rādhā, peeping through the window, Kṛishṇa was infatuated and he staggered and fell down. The confusion and noise that followed startled Kṛishṇa from the swoon. He hesitated a while, then understood and exclaimed hurriedly: "The arecanut in the betel-leaf choked me."

AFFECTED REPULSE OF ENDEARMENTS *(KUṬṬAMITA-HĀVA)*

Simulated quarrels in the midst of love-sport create *Kuṭṭamita-hāva* and add to the joy of love.

Rādhā's *Kuṭṭamita-hāva*

Simulating anger and with obstinacy she walked away, having turned her back on him. He leapt and held her again, although she struggled hard to free herself from his hold. He now pricked her flesh with his nails and teeth, and fondled her bosom, treating her worse than an enemy and transgressing all limits.

> "Now he sits by her side giving her betel-leaves to eat.
> Perverse are the ways of love, O *sakhī*."

Kṛishṇa's *Kuṭṭamita-hāva*

Seeing Kṛishṇa, Rādhā kept quiet and would not utter a word, or only say harsh things. All his requests and oaths would not make her look into his face. He entreated her timidly but in vain; he fell at her feet only to be repulsed.

> "But look now, Rādhā's face is in his lap, which he is decorating.
> The lore of love is queer."

MESSAGE THROUGH A SYMBOL (*BODHAKA-HĀVA*)

When the deep meaning of a lover's sentiment conveyed in symbols or riddles is understood by the beloved, it is said to be *Bodhaka-hāva*[11] (Figs. 28 and 29).

Rādhā's *Bodhaka-hāva*

The wise Rādhā was sitting in the midst of the assembly of her female companions, when a newly wedded cow-girl holding a faded lotus in her hand entered and fell at Rādhā's feet. Rādhā sprinkled sandal water on the lotus, offered her betel-leaf, wiped the sandal paint from her cheeks, put black paint in her eyes, and bade her good-bye.

(The stranger was a messenger from love-sick Kṛishṇa, whose plight the faded lotus symbolized. Kṛishṇa's longing for a meeting was conveyed by the messenger falling at Rādhā's feet. Rādhā secretly responded and indicated, by the wiping of sandal paint, and the application of black paint, that she would come out to meet her lover when the moon had gone down, and the night was dark.)

Kṛishṇa's *Bodhaka-hāva*

Sitting in the company of his friends and shedding his lustre around, Kṛishṇa was like the full moon surrounded by fascinated *chakoras*. A stranger entered, offered him a dripping lotus filled with fresh water, which he poured out by inverting the lotus. Kṛishṇa looked at it thoughtfully, arranged its petals into a bud, and returned it to the stranger.

(The stranger was Rādhā's messenger. The lotus filled with water signified the advent of the rainy season, which now stood between the lovers, and the drops told the story of the beloved's tears. The turning of the lotus into a bud gave the promise of meeting at night when lotuses close into buds.)

CHAPTER V

THE EIGHT HEROINES

Ashṭa Nāyikā

After describing the *nāyikās* according to personality, character and moods, as discussed in Chapter II, Keshav Dās further classifies them into the following eight types: *Svādhīnapatikā*, *Utkā*, *Vāsakasajjā*, *Abhisandhitā*, *Khaṇḍitā*, *Proshitapreyasī*, *Vipralabdhā*, and *Abhisārikā*. This classification is based on moods and situation.

Svādhīnapatikā: The loyally loved. Her husband is subject to her will.

Utkā, *Utkalā*, *Utkaṇṭhitā* or *Virahotkaṇṭhitā:* She who yearns. She expects and yearns for her lover or husband.

Vāsakasajjā: The expectant with a bed prepared. She expects her lover or husband to return from a journey, and waits with the bed prepared.

Fig. 31. The loyally loved

Abhisandhitā or *Kalahāntaritā:* The estranged by a quarrel. She repulses her husband when he seeks to soften her pride, and repents when it is already too late.

Khaṇḍitā: The sinned against. She whose husband has spent the night away from home with another woman, and reproaches him bitterly when he returns in the morning.

Proshitapatikā or *Proshitapreyasī:* She whose husband is abroad. He appoints a time of return; the day has come, but he has not yet returned.

Fig. 32. Utkā Nāyikā (Yearning for the beloved)

Vipralabdhā: The neglected. She who keeps an appointment, but night passes without her lover coming.

Abhisārikā: The forward. She goes out to seek her lover.

Sometimes the following three types are added by some rhetoricians: [12]

Pravatsyatpatikā: She who anticipates separation. She learns that her husband is about to go away on a journey at dawn.

Āgamapatikā: She whose husband is on the way home. Her happiness is increased by the news that her husband is on his way back from a far country.

Āgatapatikā: She whose husband has returned. He comes back from a journey and immediately seeks his wife.

I. SVĀDHĪNAPATIKĀ NĀYIKĀ

Svādhīnapatikā is one whose virtues her husband admires and to whom he is bound in love and is perpetually a companion. He is not henpecked, for such an idea is alien to Hindu thought, and aggressiveness is never associated with Hindu women most of whom are modest, graceful and affectionate and respect their husbands, conditioned as they are by centuries of submission and obedience.

Sakhī to Rādhā:

"O Rādhā! Kṛishṇa is the life-giver of Vraja and a darling of Brahmā; and goddesses, demon-women, Sūrya and Lakshmī are never tired of singing his praises. And you, only a mean little cow-girl, have your feet cleaned by him and he, the Lord of the Universe, is constantly clinging to you like your shadow." (Fig. 31).

"He takes care of your pettiest affairs, and protects you like betel-leaves kept in the basket and resides in you as the image dwells in the mirror. He runs after the chariot of your desires like the water of the Gaṅgā, which followed in meandering motion the chariot of Bhagīratha. Your words are like scriptures to him. It is, therefore, absurd to try to dissuade him from doing all this even for the sake of saving him from calumny."

II. UTKĀ NĀYIKĀ

Utkā is she whose anxiety is roused greatly at her lover's inability to keep his appointment with her at the promised hour (Figs. 32–35).

Nāyikā's monologue :

"Is it some business at home which detains him or the company of his friends, or is it some auspicious day of his fasting?

Was it a quarrel with some person or the dawning of divine wisdom which keeps him away from me?

Is he in pain, or is it some treachery that keeps him from meeting me, or the impeding waters, or the terrifying darkness of the night?

Or does he test my fidelity?

O my poor heart, you will never know the cause of his delay!"

Rādhā to sakhī :

"Is it his forgetfulness or has he lost the road? Is he afraid of the elements, or has he met some acquaintance on the way, or has some fair face enticed him ? Dear *sakhī*, pray see if he has come, or is still on the way, or not yet started from his place. This unending separation from Nandakumāra ! "

Utkā Nāyikā is usually represented standing or sitting upon a bed of leaves or flowers. The *Utkā* shown in a picture from Guler standing on a bed of leaves at the trysting place is very beautiful. Her slender willowy figure reclining against the trunk of the tree is an embodiment of feminine grace (Fig. 33). The *Utkā* in a painting from Kangra is standing on a bed of leaves covered with jasmine flowers. She has adorned the trunk of the tree also with garlands of jasmine. A pair of love birds in the crown of the tree heightens her loneliness. The heavy dark clouds on the village are lit up by a flash of lightning. The heroine who is like a dryad of some enchanted forest eagerly awaits the arrival of her lover (Fig. 34). Sometimes the *Utkā* is shown seated on a bed of leaves in a clump of trees. A deer is drinking water from the stream, while another is sniffing at the wind. The silence of the night is portrayed vividly (Fig. 35). The inscription on the back of the painting, translated, reads as below:

> There she sits waiting for her lover,
> Her fair body is like the white sandal tree,
> Her garments like the blue clove-vine fluttering round her fair soft limbs,
> And her lustre glows like that of a burning lamp.

Fig. 33. The anxious heroine

Fig. 34. The lady's vigil

Fig. 35. Waiting for the lover

Fig. 36. The expectant heroine

Fig. 37. Love longings (Rāginī Kāmodinī)

Fig. 38. The meeting of lovers

Excited with thoughts of her lord
She is startled by every sound of rustling leaves,
Or of birds and animals drinking the scented breeze.
Thus like a newly caged bird, she moves restlessly in her leafy nook.

III. VĀSAKASAJJĀ NĀYIKĀ

Vāsakasajjā is she, who, desirous of union with her lover, stands at the doorstep waiting for him.

"Uttering sweet words to her *sakhī* and relating to her with eagerness her heart's desire, she is casting the spell of her soft smiles, dreamy eyes and perfumed limbs. An incarnation of Rati as it were, she is as fair as a *tulasī* plant. Thus the beautiful girl, resembling *Kāntā*, adorns her bower."

Fig. 39. Vāsakasajjā Nāyikā

Vāsakasajjā Nāyikā is represented in paintings in different manners. Sometimes she is shown standing at the doorway of her bed-room expecting her lover's arrival (Fig. 36). There is an expression of eager desire in her face. She is also shown seated on a bed with garlands strewn, and lighted candles beside it (Fig. 39).

When the lovers are united, *Vāsakasajjā Nāyikā* becomes *Āgatapatikā*. The lover has returned home after long absence from a perilous journey. Overwhelmed by joy, all feelings of modesty and restraint have left her and she passionately embraces him, while a servant girl looks on, embarrassed and amused (Fig. 38).

IV. ABHISANDHITĀ NĀYIKĀ

Abhisandhitā is she who is estranged by a quarrel. She is one who disregards her lover's devotion to her, but in his absence, is full of remorse at her mistake, and the fire of separation burns her all the more. The lovers have quarrelled. The yellow-clad Kṛishṇa, with a peacock feather on his turban, is about to leave. There is intense sorrow and gloom on the face of Rādhā who has been offended at some remarks of Kṛishṇa. He has tried to soften her anger, but she does not relent, and in her anger has repulsed him. When he turns his back and is about to depart, she is sorry for her harsh conduct. Rādhā's fingers are gracefully drawn and black tresses of her hair are visible from under her transparent *dupaṭṭā*. The curves of her delicate body, her pencilled eyebrows and her mood of resentment and sorrow are eloquently portrayed in this painting (Fig. 40).

Fig. 40. Lovers' quarrel

Rādhā soliloquizes:

"How foolish of me not to have responded to him when he spoke to me repeatedly! I was adamant and would not yield to him when he came and fell at my feet. And now my limbs seem to be dissolving like butter with excitement. Woe to me, my helplessness defies all cures! Shutting out all feeling of love, I was obstinate to him without whom I have not the power to live! How unlucky that when he tried to propitiate me, I didn't acquiesce; and this gives to my soul the bitterest mortification and repentance."

Thus says *nāyikā* to *sakhī:*

"*Sakhī*, when he fell at my feet, I turned my eyes away

Fig. 41. The offended heroine

Fig. 42. The lady in grief

from him. I took my lessons from the God of Anger, and I didn't act upon your advice. And, now, all joys have turned into woes. Sandal-paste, the rays of the moon, breezes from the Yamunā's bank, and lotuses all burn my body. Since I reversed the sacred code of justice, all good things have reversed their effect upon me."

V. KHAṆḌITĀ NĀYIKĀ

Khaṇḍitā is the sinned against. She is one whose lover, having promised to come at night, does not come and turns up at her house the next morning after spending the night with another woman.

The *nāyikā* knows that the *nāyaka's* eyes are red because he kept awake the whole night in the house of some woman. But she questions him adroitly because of the presence of her *sakhīs* before whom she doesn't want to raise a serious dispute.

"Mohan, slightly different from what they were before, your eyes seem as if coloured with *mahāvar* paint. Tell me on oath if they are so red on account of anger or with amorous excitement. They look bewitched, but still they bewitch me. Are they burning in the flames of separation from me, or in the fire of some other woman's love?"

In the pictures of the *Khaṇḍitā Nāyikā* the lover is shown entering the courtyard of *nāyikā's* house, abashed with a sense of guilt on his face, and the angry and offended *nāyikā* is upbraiding him (Fig. 41).

VI. PROSHITAPREYASĪ NĀYIKĀ

Proshitapreyasī is one whose husband has gone away from her for some period on some

Fig. 43. Proshitapreyasī Nāyikā

business, and has not returned on the appointed day. Hence she is sad and worried, and is not consoled, though her companion tries to comfort her (Fig. 43).

Thus says *sakhī* to *nāyikā*: "How delightful is this auspicious day of your lord's return—perhaps it is the fruit of many virtuous deeds done in the past! This day has as if unexpectedly arrived, for who could say that he wouldn't have had to stay away for some more days? But why don't you smile as you speak on this exceedingly charming day which does not seem to thrill you? Your obstinacy is indeed hard as wood, and no fire of separation could burn it."

VII. VIPRALABDHĀ NĀYIKĀ

Vipralabdhā is the disappointed heroine, who has waited in vain for her lover the whole night through. The *vipralabdhā* is shown standing under a tree at the edge of a bed of leaves, tearing off her ornaments in disgust and flinging them on the ground. The empty space in the background symbolises the loneliness of the lady, her frustration and deep distress (Fig. 44). It is thus that the *nāyikā's* feelings are described by her confidante:

"Flowers are like arrows, fragrance becomes ill-odour, pleasant bowers like fiery furnaces,

Gardens are like the wild woods, Ah Keśava, the moon rays burn her body as though with fever,

Love like a tiger holds her heart, no watch of the night brings any gladness,

Songs have the sound of abuse, *pān* has the taste of poison, every jewel burns like a firebrand."

Fig. 44. Vipralabdhā Nāyikā

Fig. 45. The neglected

Fig. 46. Abhisārikā Nāyikā

Fig. 47. The lady goes to meet her lover in a dark night

VIII. ABHISĀRIKĀ NĀYIKĀ

Abhisārikā is the forward. She is one who goes out to meet her lover from love, pride or desire (Plate VII).

Abhisārikā is of three types:

Premābhisārikā who accosts her lover with affection and feeling of love.
Garvābhisārikā is one who accosts her lover with pride and vanity.
Kāmābhisārikā is one who accosts her lover with lustful passion.

There is yet another threefold classification:

Svakīyā-abhisārikā is she, who, with her limbs decorated with ornaments, out of excessive modesty, goes out with unsteady steps in the company of wedded women.

Parakīyā-abhisārikā walks coyly on the road, and thus illumines the company of her friends kinswomen and other women.

Sāmānyā-abhisārikā: With a bewildered mind but possessing courage, with her body clad in blue garments and limbs beautified by paints, perfumes and ornaments, she goes out at twilight and on festivals at midnight with her friends, and holding flower covered branches in her hand, looks on all sides, smiles, and wins the hearts of men with her gracefulness.

An *abhisārikā* has gone out to meet her lover, and the following conversation takes place between them:

Nāyaka: "You have enslaved me, dear, by coming here even though not called."
Nāyikā: "But, Ghanaśyāma, clouds came and brought me here."
Nāyaka: "I can't even see your body in this darkness. I wonder how you found the way."
Nāyikā: "Lightning showed me the path."
Nāyaka: "But your feet must have been hurt on the uneven path covered with mud and thorns."
Nāyikā: "The elephant of courage which I was riding was very comfortable indeed."
Nāyaka: "How did you dare come absolutely alone in this dark and horrible night?"
Nāyikā: "Your love was my companion."

Sakhī to *nāyaka* on seeing the *nāyikā* who has come out to meet him:

"The longing in her eyes, the art of her speech, and the fairness of her limbs cannot remain hidden nor can the majesty of her gait. A *chitriṇī* cow-girl is with her, and her matchless form betrays her mind. Her delightful yearnings—sublime like the moon—are soaring high as if on the palanquins of your fawn-like eyes. Discard your anxiety and take your drink and meal peacefully; for it is the same charming cow-girl whom you saw yesterday."

"Her fine garments are perfumed with sandal; necklaces are decorating her bosom, and her flower-ornaments are as if the repository of all bliss. I would gladly sacrifice crores of Ratis to have a glimpse of her. She is playing upon her *vīṇā*, and fawns and swans are gambolling round her, and she looks like Sarasvatī. Forgetting the darkness and the

Fig. 48. The forward

pain of separation, her eyes, fond like those of a *chakora* are beaming with joy. The captivating beauty of this pair of moons is bewildering her rivals and sweeping them off their feet. Their yellow sparkle is fading them as if they were lotuses confronting the moon."

A *sakhī* is telling another how the *nāyikā* crossed the wood at night to meet her lover:

"Serpents were coiling round her legs and their heads were being crushed beneath her feet; and evil spirits ranging abroad, could be seen in all directions. She didn't notice the torrential rain, nor the terrifying thunder of dark clouds, nor the screaming of cicadas amidst the roaring of the storm. She didn't know when her ornaments fell off one by one. Defying the ditches and brambles that tried to stand in her way, she went on. The goblin-wives themselves wondered and are asking her, 'Wherefrom have you learnt this *yoga*-like *abhisāra*? Oh *Abhisārikā*, how marvellous this trysting!' " (Fig. 46).

A *sakhī* tries to dissuade a *nāyikā* who, burning with passion, is ready to dart forth to meet her lord in spite of impediments:

"O foolish girl, don't you know that many aged cowherds are sitting on the way, and that scores of assemblies are in progress? Streets are overcrowded with playful urchins who will win any girl's heart. Many women are going this way and that, and they, though hiding their faces in their veils, can recognize the very shadow of others. Displaying your moon-like face, where are you hastening? Are you in your right mind?"

There is yet another classification of *Abhisārikā:*

Sandhyābhisārikā, who visits her beloved in the evening twilight.
Kṛishṇābhisārikā, who does so on dark nights (Fig. 47).
Śuklābhisārikā, who does so on bright moonlit nights.
Divābhisārikā, who does so by day.

According to the *Kāma-sūtra*, desire in the heart of a woman waxes and wanes with the moon. When the full moon spreads its magical radiance over the landscape in the Kangra Valley, the valley gets transformed into a fairy land. Under the magic of moonlight, harsh details of the landscape fade, a voluptuous repose descends on Nature, and the crowns of the mango, *pīpal* and pine trees melt into the mountains, appearing like lovers united. In the light of the moon the lovers go out in search of each other. In a Kangra painting, a lady is shown going in search of her lover. There is a full moon in the sky filling the atmosphere with its silvery beams. The pale light of the moon, cool and phosphorescent, is painted with remarkable skill. The lady is *śuklābhisārikā* who goes out to seek her lover. The drapery of the woman and her delicate features are suffused with mellow light (Plate VIII).

CHAPTER VI

LOVE IN SEPARATION

Vipralambha

PŪRVĀNURĀGA

Keshav Dās defines *Vipralambha Śṛiṅgāra*, as the sentiment aroused by the separation of lovers. The sentiment of love in separation is determined by four conditions:

Pūrvānurāga: the beginning of love.

Māna: separation on account of coldness or obstinacy.

Pravāsa: separation of lovers in different places or countries. (As on the departure of Kṛishṇa from Vṛindāvana to Mathurā.)

Karuṇā: death.

Pūrvānurāga is the beginning of love and the awakening of desire for union. The beloved may be seen in a dream, in a picture or in real life. As the *gopīs* said to Kṛishṇa, 'Love is born in the eyes, is fed by gazing, and is sealed into an entity through courtship and

Fig. 49. A glimpse of the beloved

love-talks'. Love in India is always love at first sight, as of Hīr and Rāñjhā, and Sohnī and Mahīwāl, on the pattern of Dante and Beatrice. The meeting of the eyes may take place at the village well when the thirsty wayfarer asks for water, at the bathing *ghāṭ*, at a festival, or at a religious gathering.

The sentiments of love at first sight are described with utmost charm in the sparkling love poems of Vidyāpati, who thus describes the *pūrvānurāga* of Kṛishṇa for Rādhā:

Kṛishṇa: "Why did that moon-face cross my path?
Whose sidelong glance is all too keen:
An ill day that for me!

My thoughts were set upon her breasts,
Love lay waking in my heart,
Her voice was ringing in my ears;
I would have gone, my feet refused to move.

The bonds of hope constrain me yet;
Love is a tide, says Vidyāpati."[13]

There are a number of paintings illustrating *pūrvānurāga* in the *Nāyaka-Nāyikā* as well as *Rāgamālā* series. Meeting at the village well or bathing *ghāṭ* is a familiar theme. Kṛishṇa has a glimpse of the charm of Rādhā when she has just finished her bath, and is busy with her coiffure (Plate IX). There are a number of paintings representing the *nāyikā* at her bath. In some of the pictures showing bathing scenes, which are the most charming products of the Kangra School, the lover is not shown, and the lady alone is depicted after her bath on a terrace (Plate X).

The poet thus describes the beauty of Rādhā at her bath:

"Once on a time the daughter of Vṛishabhānu rose from her bed and came out on the terrace to bathe, O *sakhī!*

Her body shone through the shimmering bodice like the reflection of the moon in the waters of the Yamunā.

The long locks hanging from her head in lovely wise curled back upon her breasts,

Whereat the river spake, 'There has come some serpent to worship Śiva in the shape of the fair moon's image'."[14]

There are a number of paintings of bathing beauties in which the artists fully avail themselves of the opportunity of displaying feminine charm. A woman, seated on a *chaukī*, her bust projecting, and arms raised, is wringing her wet hair (Fig. 50). The poet compares the stream of water pouring from her hair to a dark cloud scattering strings of pearls. Sometimes a swan is shown drinking the falling drops of water.

In another painting Rādhā has finished her bath, and seated on a *chaukī* is looking into a mirror attended by her maidens. Kṛishṇa, taking full advantage of the opportunity, is looking from a window (Fig. 49). The lover may have an opportunity of seeing the charm of the beloved when she is playing with a yo-yo, and is crossing the courtyard of the house. While she is flitting across the courtyard, her *dupaṭṭā* slips from her head. She looks

Fig. 50. Lady bathing

Fig. 51. Detail of Fig. 49

up and sees her lover, their eyes meet, and her sweet glance shows her innermost thought (Plate XI). A glimpse may be had of the beloved while occupied with her household work. Rādhā is in the kitchen stirring a pot on the fire while Kṛishṇa is talking to her confidante on the terrace. In some of the pictures showing cooking scenes, while Rādhā is busy in the kitchen, Kṛishṇa is shown standing secretly near a window watching her beauty spellbound.

"The Sweetheart's bosom came forth, and all her body shone with beauty — as if to watch the stirring of the lentils, that her garments hid."[15]

In Chapter VIII of the *Rasikapriyā*, Keshav Dās thus defines *pūrvānurāga:* "When the lovers deprived of the sight of each other's comely form, which produces love, suffer pain, *pūrvānurāga* becomes manifest."

Rādhā's Secret *Pūrvānurāga*

Nāyikā to sakhī: "Don't show me flowers, which, without Kṛishṇa, give pain like thorns. Take away the garland which looks like a serpent. Don't shake the *chāmar* nor the fan, because the perfumed air only makes me mad. Don't apply sandal-paste, because it only causes fever. Keep saffron away, for it seems to kindle fire within me. Don't give betel-leaves to me for they taste like poison. You must be mad not to heed my requests."

Rādhā's Manifested *Pūrvānurāga*

Nāyikā to sakhī: "Since the day I somehow looked at the object of my desire, my mind has fallen into a state which cannot be described. If you talk about me or my condition to others I shall be laughed at. Knowing you as my wellwisher I have come to ask you for the remedy. How shall I meet him; and, without meeting him, how shall I live? There is love in my eyes, but fear in my heart."

Kṛishṇa's Secret *Pūrvānurāga*

Nāyaka to sakhī: "Once Rādhā was sitting with her mother in the company of her friends. Passing by, I saw her, and she gave me an indescribable look expressive of her love. Since that day the talk of all other women sounds like crude prattle. My mind has wandered everywhere, but it has not seen another such beauty."

Kṛishṇa's Manifested *Pūrvānurāga*

Nāyaka to sakhī: "Ever since Rādhā united her gaze with mine, and drew my eyes to her, enslaving them with her laughter and her raised eyebrows, the sight of other women gives me no pleasure. They stifle longings and cause pain, as the *chakorī*, in separation from moonlight, swallows live embers."

CHAPTER VII

LOVE IN SEPARATION

Māna

Māna is separation of lovers on account of jealousy, obduracy, pride, impropriety of speech or conduct, or coldness. *Māna* may be slight *(laghu)*, moderate *(madhyama)*, or heavy *(guru)*. Mystically interpreted, *Māna* is the intrusion of ego which stands between the union of the soul and God. Vidyāpati, Keshav Dās and Bihārī Lāl have all described the *Māna* of Rādhā in their works. In *Kṛishṇa Avatāra*, Guru Govind Singh has given a very moving account of the *Māna* of Rādhā. There are a number of paintings of *Māninī Nāyikās* in Kangra art, which are mostly illustrations of the poetry of Keshav Dās and Bihārī. Out of these, three are reproduced in this book, viz. Plate XIII and Figs. 52 and 54.

Keshav Dās defines *Māna* as the sentiment of pride, which is aroused by the fullness of love, and which heightens its glory.

GURU MĀNA

On seeing the evidence of another woman's presence or on hearing her name, *Guru Māna* becomes manifest.

Rādhā's Secret *Guru Māna*

"Forgetting his quarrel with Rādhā, Kṛishṇa met her and revelled in the enchantment of her beauty, love and laughter. On seeing nail-marks on his person beneath his garment, she turned her gaze away, and her eyes drooped like a lotus flower at the sight of the moon." (Nail-marks resemble the crescent moon.)

Rādhā's Manifested *Guru Māna*

Rādhā asked Kṛishṇa to narrate stories to her. While he was doing that, the name of another woman escaped his lips unawares. On hearing it, the betel-leaf in her mouth and the one in her hand which she was about to offer him remained where they were, and tears rolled down her eyes.

Nāyaka's *Guru Māna*

When the *nāyikā* speaks words that transgress the bounds of propriety, *Guru Māna* is aroused in the mind of the *nāyaka*.

Kṛishṇa's Secret *Guru Māna*

Rādhā: "O Kṛishṇa, you are false to your vows and your loves are now being disclosed. Come and see this love-letter which has been found in your turban. Though written on ordinary paper, it is like a blazing furnace to me. This is the road to infamy. Only God knows how many such roads you have traversed! Why do you compel me, by your conduct, to utter words bitter as poison?"

To this Kṛishṇa replied laughingly: "To me these words sound sweet."

Kṛishṇa's Manifested *Guru Māna*

Sakhī to nāyikā: "If you have a complaint against your dear one, you should speak of it only in private to him; it would be wrong to disclose his guilts publicly. If his eyes stray in undesirable directions, you may try to restrain them, but not to prick them with a knife. Remember, he is the same Śyāma, separation from whom can kindle such a fire in the hearts of women that a solution of camphor will have to be sprayed to cool it. You should speak as propriety demands, and not speak harshly to one who has abandoned everything for the sake of your love."

LAGHU MĀNA

When the *nāyikā* herself sees the *nāyaka* looking at another woman, or hears from her *sakhī* of such conduct of the *nāyaka*, *Laghu Māna* is manifested.

Rādhā's Secret *Laghu Māna*

"O Kṛishṇa, the wisdom of your beloved one and the purity of her innocence remain

Fig.52. The obstinacy of Rādhā

locked up in her mind. I cannot say if she is feeling proud or insulted. Who can know whether she is pained or amused, fascinated or furious? Her replies are neither refusal nor affirmation, and her composure alternates with impulsiveness — she changes like the shadow of shifting clouds."

Rādhā's Manifested *Laghu Māna*

Sakhī : "Even the pretence of annoyance with the dear one is unworthy, and such indifference is indeed unimaginable."

Nāyikā : "Who is dear, if he is himself indifferent?"

Sakhī : "Only yesterday he was sending his messages of solicitude through me."

Nāyikā : "Why did you not come yesterday, if you profess goodness?"

Sakhī : "Today I offer to act as a truce-maker."

Nāyikā : "It seems you will only cause a breach, for I am disillusioned by the deeds of Kṛishṇa, who like a *kanera* bud is white within, though red without."

Sakhī : "Is there a witness who can be asked to verify this accusation?"

Nāyikā : "I would need no witness, for I have seen things myself."

Fig. 53. Detail of Fig. 52

When the *nāyikā* does not act according to the *nāyaka's* bidding, *Laghu Māna* becomes manifest in his mind.

Kṛishṇa's Secret *Laghu Māna*

"I don't know what you will do in future. Already you have caused such pain by not doing your beloved's bidding. Out of modesty you avoided expression of your affection and thus caused injury to love. You did not hold him in your arms, nor did you amuse him with the novelty of your speech, nor indeed did you gaze at him as if filling your eyes with his appearance. Why have you turned your mind away from him?"

Rādhā's Manifested *Laghu Māna*

"What wrong have I done to you that you do not speak to me as you used to do in the past? How would I know what is hidden in your heart unless I hear of it? Strange is your appetite, for you do not know how to cool the boiling milk before drinking it, nor let the grapes ripen on the vine before tasting them. Rightly are you called Kuñjavihārī!"

Fig. 54. The obdurate

(Kuñjavihārī also means a monkey. The reference is to *nāyaka's* premature desire for the *nāyikā* who is still too young for love, and to his monkey-like impulsiveness to taste unripe fruit. His *laghu māna* has been caused by the *nāyikā's* refusal to make love.)

MADHYAMA MĀNA

When the *nāyikā* sees the *nāyaka* talking to another woman, *Madhyama Māna* is aroused.

Rādhā's Secret *Madhyama Māna*

Nāyikā: "Say, where did you spend the whole night?"

Nāyaka: "In waiting for you."

Nāyikā: "What are these marks on your body?"

Nāyaka: "These are scratches made by thorns during my wanderings in the forest."

Nāyikā: "Why these red eyes?"

Nāyaka: "Because of having burnt in the fire of your separation."

Seeing her winning grace, the *nāyaka* embraced her.

Rādhā's Manifested *Madhyama Māna*

Nāyikā to the other woman: "Have you come to indulge in your prattle as you do so immodestly in his presence? I cannot say what I wanted to say, for I do not wish to narrate unabashedly my secret shame. If Kṛishṇa has been so shameless, I cannot tread in his footsteps."

When the high-minded *nāyikā* cannot be brought round by the *nāyaka*, who, having failed, gives up the attempt, *Madhyama Māna* is aroused in his mind.

Kṛishṇa's Secret *Madhyama Māna*

Sakhī to nāyikā: "I tried to dissuade you from showing pride to Kṛishṇa, and you refused to listen to his solicitous words. O lotus-faced one, now look at your faded face in the mirror. All your *sakhīs* had given advice to you in the interest of your welfare, but you never listened. I know that one day you would have to send me to Kṛishṇa to propitiate him."

Kṛishṇa's Manifested *Madhyama Māna*

Sakhī to nāyikā: "O high-minded girl, you should come round if besought with respect. If you would not, you would be left only with your pride, for the lover would become disgusted with you. He would also talk slightingly of you in the presence of other women. I had advised you to be reconciled when he was begging you to forgive him, for otherwise you would have to go a-begging to seek reconciliation with him."

RECONCILIATION OF LOVERS

Women have an insatiable need for love and tenderness, and reconciliation follows when the hero says sweet words, or gives her a gift, or expresses regret at his conduct and gives an assurance of loyalty and love to the beloved. Sometimes *sakhīs* are won over by the *nāyaka* and they prevail upon the *nāyikā* to relent. Sometimes out of desire for pleasure, the *nāyaka* falls at the feet of the *nāyikā* and thus wins her over. When this happens the tactful *nāyaka* does not mention her *Māna*, and instead talks of other matters.

In re-union the lovers give up their pride in six ways, namely, *Sāma* (gentle advice), *Dāna* (gift), *Bheda* (dissension), *Praṇati* (falling at feet), *Upekshā* (neglect), and *Prasaṅga-vidhvaṁsa* (change of topic).

Gentle Advice

Sāma-upāya of Rādhā

Nāyaka to nāyikā: "One who hopes for joy, should not be given pain. One who has been accepted as your own should not be made the object of annoyance. You and I are one entity — two bodies with one soul. Pride is the root of disaffection, and should not, therefore, be thought of even in a dream."

Sāma-upāya of Kṛishṇa

Nāyikā to nāyaka: "People are talking against us, because of your conduct; otherwise they would not do that. Why follow a tiresome and thorny track? When people will raise an

Fig. 55. Kṛishṇa offering a garland of flowers to Rādhā

accusing finger at you, our love will pine away like the tender sprout of *regma* creeper. You must, therefore, act wisely, for you and I are indeed inseparable."

Gift

Where a gift is accepted out of greed and pride is given up, a harlot's characteristics are manifested.

Dāna-upāya of Kṛishṇa

Sakhī, carrying nāyaka's gift of a garland of 'bandhu-jīva' flowers, to nāyikā: "Look at the soft spotless petals of these flowers as if newly created by Brahmā. These red flowers are dear to the Sun, their lord. Their redness can be compared to the sweetest and loveliest of lips. They have all qualities except fragrance. And having heard of and now seen your bosom, which resembles the Malaya mountain, covered by curling tresses which are like the snakes on mountains, they long to become fragrant by a touch of your bosom. Will you just wear them round your neck?"

Sakhī, presenting to nāyikā a necklace of ivory beads sent as a gift by nāyaka: "When this ivory was a part of the wild elephant's tusk, it had rent living creatures and inanimate objects alike. Since that time it is being tortured by fate in many ways; it has been pierced with holes and tied up in a string. To wash away its sins, this necklace has now thought of a pilgrimage to your bosom, the seat of holiness."

Dāna-upāya of Rādhā

Rādhā came smilingly to Kṛishṇa and sang to him a tale of love. She then asked him to explain to her the meaning of some of the sequences of the story: the simultaneous partaking by the lovers of the nectar of each other's mouths, and of other parts of the body which in consequence suffered amorous injuries by nails and teeth. Enclosing him in an embrace, she also asked him, on an oath, what mode of embracing the lovers in the tale had adopted. Thus did Rādhā herself make up her quarrel with her lover today.

Dissension

Bheda-upāya of Rādhā

Sakhī, who has been won over by nāyaka, to nāyikā: "The nurse and the servant, out of self-interest, are hesitating to give you counsel; but destiny has so bound me to you that I cannot help but give you my advice. Please speak gently lest your harsh words should pierce the soft heart of Kṛishṇa."

Bheda-upāya of Kṛishṇa

Sakhī, who has been won over by nāyikā, to Kṛishṇa: "Having been told by someone that you were angry with her, Rādhā has been straining her mind to devise some means of reconciliation without becoming a laughing stock, but her thinking has been of no avail. The poor girl is between two fires: your anger and the taunts of jealous women. I ask you now if she should come to propitiate you."

Falling at Feet

Praṇati-upāya of Rādhā (Out of love)

Nāyikā to sakhī : "All of them are saying about me that even when Kṛishṇa came and held my feet and thus demonstrated his love for me, I did not look straight at him. They are as if making a stream of calumny flow against me. I ask you with all humility to say whether, when Kṛishṇa came to propitiate me, I insulted him or merely displayed my self-respect."

Praṇati-upāya of Rādhā (Out of lust)

Sakhī to nāyikā : "If you wouldn't speak yourself, you should respond when spoken to. Why must you let me wear out my heart with unresponded talking. Kṛishṇa, for whose sake all the young women of Vraja would give their soul, has knelt at your feet. Give up your obstinacy and press him to your heart. How long will you remain stiff, and continue looking at the sky arrogantly? Each day has become unbearably long like two days because of this estrangement; but your thinking is still perverse."

Praṇati-upāya of Rādhā (Out of guilt)

"You spent the whole day in utter dejection and mental pain. When night fell, your *sakhīs* pleaded with you till midnight. The counsel of the friends as well as of your nurse was of no avail. Why did you not come round, O high-minded lady, till your lover came and fell at your feet?"

Nāyikā falls at the feet of *nāyaka* to propitiate him only out of love. Such a solicitation is not made out of lust or from a sense of guilt, because that would mean violation of *rasa.*

Praṇati-upāya of Kṛishṇa

Sakhī to nāyaka : "Water can do without the fish, but the fish can live only in water. For the sake of her, without whom previously nothing appeared tasteful, you should do what would please her. You used to fall at my feet to get united to her; and now, why don't you raise her to your bosom when she is at your feet? Is there anyone who would even dream of barring the door against the approaching Lakshmī? Pray, take my advice."

Neglect

Upekshā-upāya of Rādhā

Sakhī to nāyikā : "This is not the flash of lightning but of weapons. This is not the sound of peacocks, but of the bards singing praises of heroes. It is not the thunder of clouds but of the war-drums. The sun has as if covered his face out of fear. O damsel with a moon-like face, hasten to your friend Kṛishṇa, who is the destroyer of enemies, for these clouds, which are the warriors of the Demon of Darkness, are coursing on the horses of high winds in search of the moon."

Upekshā-upāya of Kṛishṇa

Sakhī to nāyaka : "Look at the conduct of this shameless bumble bee who, in the company of his spouse, goes to woo *mālatī.* He admires day and night the colours of *ketakī*; in his heart resides *chamelī* and in his eyes *nalinī*. He drinks the juice from *mādhavī*, and tastes the *sevatī* simultaneously with the *champā*."

"Why are you feeling ashamed like a person with a guilty mind, for I have to say more yet."

Change of Topic

Prasaṅga-Vidhvaṃsa-upāya of Rādhā

Sakhī to nāyikā: "O *sakhī*, these are not peacocks but the servants of Kāmadeva who roam about and give the warning that if any love-lorn maiden shows obstinacy, she would incur the displeasure of the God of Love. These thundering clouds are in fact his drum-beaters heralding the joys of love. You may get angry again in the morning; but you should call Kṛishṇa now and tell him about these announcements of the God of Love."

Prasaṅga-Vidhvaṃsa-upāya of Kṛishṇa

Sakhī to nāyaka: "You have tutored your parrot so well that he is not talking to his mate. He is instead teaching the lore of love to *sārikā* and has secretly increased his love fourfold; so has his pride increased too. His poor hesitant mate is pining away. She cannot tell her tale of woe to anyone. Her body burns in anguish. In spite of this shameless arrogance, the parrot is unreconciled. Now go and settle their quarrel which has small reason."

(The pining mate and the danger to her life cause fear and take away the *nāyaka's* pride.)

Pride can be easily dispelled by clever words, by proper time and place, by sweet words, sweet music, beautiful sights, and sweet fragrance.

Without pleading for either side, the pride of the lovers gets broken and their hearts swell for union at the sound of thundering clouds, shouting of peacocks and the buzzing of bees; at the sight of flashing lightning, radiant limbs, a decorated bed and a beautiful garden; by the smell of saffron, camphor and flowers.

Thus do the lovers take away each other's pride and enhance their love.

The beloved should not display excessive pride for, if the lover becomes indifferent, he would be lost to the beloved.

Pride may be shown occasionally, but not frequently, so that mutual regard grows.

According to the tradition of *Māna*, there can be no love without fear, nor any fear without love.

The *nāyikā* becomes indifferent to the *nāyaka* because of his conceit, vice, loss of wealth, harsh words, living in a far-off place, greed and unpleasant deeds.

CHAPTER VIII

LOVE IN SEPARATION

Pravāsa

Pravāsa is the separation of lovers in different places or countries, and is the third phase of *viraha*. It is exemplified in the departure of Kṛishṇa from Vṛindāvana to Mathura, when the *gopīs* became extremely anxious and sent him messages of their love-sickness. Mystically interpreted, *pravāsa* corresponds to what the Christian mystics of Europe call the Dark Night of the Soul. The feeling of desolation and grief of a woman separated from her husband is universal. Grief of a Japanese *virahiṇī nāyikā* is thus described in a famous Japanese poem, 'Crows at Twilight' in *Ritaihaku:*

> "Athwart the yellow clouds of sunset, seeking their nests under the city wall,
> The crows fly homeward. Caw! Caw! they cry among the branches.
> At her loom sits weaving silk brocade, one like the Lady of Shinsen:
> Their voices come to her through the window with its curtains misty-blue.
> She stays the shuttle; grieving, she thinks of her far-distant lord:
> In the lonely, empty room, her tears fall like rain."[16]

In folk-songs and ballads from the Kangra Valley there are vivid descriptions of the distress of the lonely wife separated from her husband. Her tresses, so lovingly scented and combed with sandal-combs, are now dishevelled. She no longer paints the beauty spot on her forehead, and feels no joy in wearing ornaments. Her clothes are shabby and coarse. She has forgotten her pets, the *chakoras*, peacocks and geese. Even Nature is in sympathy with her in her sorrow, and as she weeps, mountains and rivers share her grief, and trees too drop their leaves as a token of sympathy. For her, it seems, as if time has stood still, and the long nights of winter months tarry and hesitate as if unwilling to depart. In the months of March and April the mangoes flower, *koels* shout day and night, but these only add to her anguish. In spring while other women are happy with their husbands, the lonely wife, tormented by her loneliness, thus gives vent to her feelings:

> List, the *koels* sing!
> In the mango grove,
> I, my raiment not yet unbound,
> Have to sleep alone.

In the month of May, mango blossoms ripen into green fruits but she is unhappy. In June the mangoes fully ripen on the boughs of trees but they bring her no joy. In the months of July and August rain falls day and night, and her tears also fall like rain. The nights of September and October lighted by the moon are so bright that one can see even the bottom of the lotus-filled lake, but to her they look dark and dismal. She asks the rivers, clouds, and birds and beasts of the forest to be witnesses to her sorrow, and to carry the message of her grief-filled heart to her lover. It is thus that her desolation is described in a folk-song from Kangra:

If the bodice is torn it can be mended

If the sky bursts, how can you sew it?

While the poets of the West have written about the love of man for woman, it is the poets of the East who have sung of the love of woman for man. Vidyāpati thus describes the state of Rādhā in separation from Kṛishṇa who has gone to Mathura from Gokula:

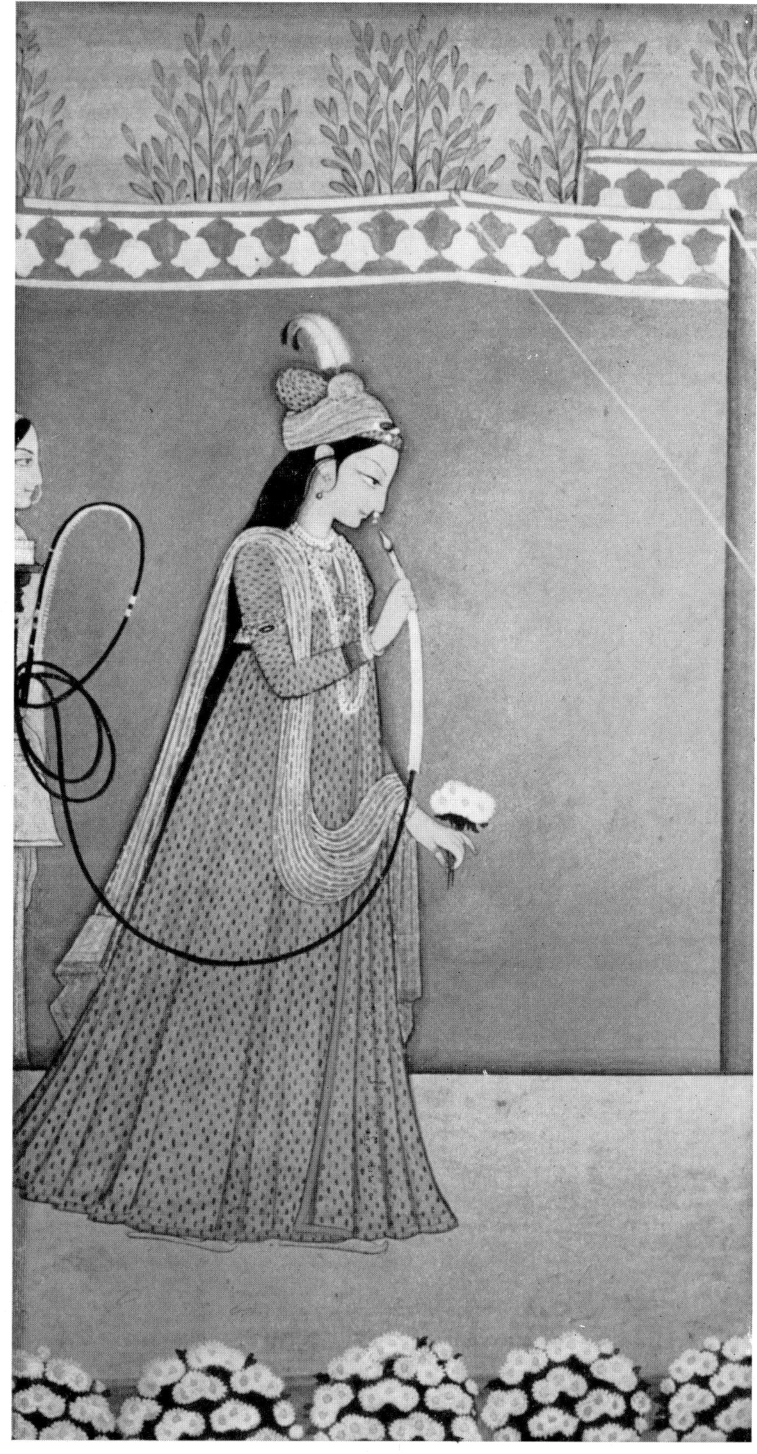

Fig. 56. Longings of love

Rādhā:
"Now Mādhava has gone to Mathura town,
(Who can have stolen the jewel of Gokula?)
Gokula resounds with the noise of weeping,
See how the waves are swollen with tears!

Empty the temple, empty the lover,
Empty each airt, empty all!
How can I go to Yamunā's bank?
How can I look on the booths and groves?

How can I look on the place and live,
Where he smothered my friends with flowers?"[17]

Autumn rains give happiness to lovers who are together. They enjoy the rumble of the clouds and the play of lightning. Even birds and animals are happy but not Rādhā. Vidyāpati thus describes her feelings:

Rādhā:

"There is no limit to my woe, my dear!
O heavy rains of autumn tide,
My house is empty!

Impenetrable clouds are thundering unceasingly,
And all the world is full of rain:
Kanta is a stone, and Love is cruel,
A rain of arrows pierces me.

A hundred flashes blind my eyes,
The peacock dances in an ecstasy:
The happy frogs but croak and croak,
My heart is bursting.

Utter darkness, night impenetrable,
Unbroken line of lightning;
Vidyāpati says: How may you pass
The day and night alone?"[18]

Seeing the condition of Rādhā, her confidante arrives at Mathura, and thus describes her grief to Kṛishṇa:

Dūtikā:

"Mādhava, O moon-face,
Never can you have known the sting of separation!
Hearing you are departed to another land, she wastes away:
O wretched Rāi, bereft of wit by force of love!

Refusing even buds of flowers, she lies exhausted on the ground
The calling of the *koel* fills her with fear,
Her tears have washed the beauty-spots away,
Her wasted arms let slip their ornaments.

With hanging head Rādhā regards her throat,
Now are her fingers raw with writing on the ground:
Says Vidyāpati: Recollecting all his ways,
And taking count of them, she fainted."[19]

From among the creations of the Kangra School it is the paintings of love-lorn women, *virahiṇī nāyikās*, which are most touching. The lover has gone on a journey and in his absence his beloved suffers from the pangs of separation. To her, though surrounded by her *sakhīs*, the house looks empty, and she feels desolate. The Kangra artists have poignantly portrayed in their paintings of *virahiṇī nāyikās* the pathos which lies in the silent depths of a woman's heart in all its tragic intensity. Lonely women standing on the sills of door-frames wistfully looking at clouds and lightning, clasping smooth trunks of plantains, holding the branch of a tree, carrying fans and cooling the fever of love in a moonlit night, or escaping a storm and hurrying inside rooms are all love-sick women. Solitary women with pets like black-bucks, parrots, *chakoras* and pigeons are also love-lorn women, the male animals and birds being the symbols of the absent lover. A *nāyikā* watches pensively the amorous sports of a pair of pigeons. This painting is a representation of *smaraṇa*, the remembrance of past union (Fig. 67). A number of these paintings are illustrations of situations from Chapter VIII of the *Rasikapriyā*. Keshav Dās thus describes the ten states of love in separation:

TEN STATES OF LOVE IN SEPARATION

(Daśa Daśās)

The desire for union springs from seeing the beloved one and hearing him. When the desire to meet him is not fulfilled, ten conditions result therefrom, namely, longing *(abhilāsha)*, anxiety *(chintā)*, reminiscence *(smṛiti)*, the recalling of the qualities of the beloved one *(guṇa-kathana)*, agitation *(udvega)*, delirium *(pralāpa)*, sickness *(vyādhi)*, stupor *(jaḍatā)*, derangement *(unmāda)*, and death *(maraṇa)*.

Longing *(Abhilāsha)*

When eyes, speech and minds are united, bodies also wish to unite. Such, indeed, is *abhilāsha!*

Rādhā's Longing (Secret)

Sakhī to nāyikā: "Your wisdom and discernment are waning; the radiance of your limbs has gone although it should have increased day by day. The anguish of your heart which you conceal is being betrayed by your face. You have forgotten your joys and hunger and sleep. Your heart's desires are looking for a prop. It seems as if you have lost something; your inner being seems to be aflame, and in your restlessness you are straying here and there."

Rādhā's Longing (Manifested)

Nāyikā to sakhī: "Seeing him once may arouse an insatiable longing to see him always; this will fill all my days with pain. Instead, I shall see him in my heart (or imagining), and seeing him thus in secret shall see him more and more, and yet not let him see my physical appearance. You are coaxing me with empty promises to let me see him; I know your promises cannot help."

Kṛishṇa's Longing (Secret)

Sakhī to nāyaka: "I beg of you not to confide in others and share your secret thoughts with them, nor thus to bring infamy to her name as you have done to your own. For days on end, you may have to go without seeing her, seeing whom for a whole day does not satiate you. See that you do not burn yourself in your eagerness to drink hot milk; you must let it cool."

Kṛishṇa's Longing (Manifested)

Sakhī to another sakhī: "Is there any wellwisher of his, who would ask him which way he is drifting? Quite naturally are the ill-famed women of Gokula slandering the chaste ones; such has been his conduct! Look, how he is staring at us and asks who I am, as if he does not know one who only yesterday was delivering to him the message from his beloved."

Anxiety *(Chintā)*

The feeling of *chintā* comes when the lover thinks of how to meet the beloved one, and having met, how to win her.

Rādhā's Anxiety (Secret)

Nāyikā to herself: "How shall I make him my slave, seeing whom I lose control over my own self (body)?"

Rādhā's Anxiety (Manifested)

Sakhī to nāyaka: "Since she saw you, her mental state has been like the cross-moves in a game of chess — the kings being love and fear, the queens being reason and hesitation; the bishops being separation and dalliance, the knights being the glances of her eyes; the rooks her desires, and the pawns the sixteen ways of ornamentation. There is fierce pressure from both sides. Let us see which side comes out victorious."

Kṛishṇa's Anxiety (Secret)

Nāyaka to himself: "When will she, whose body is the abode of all fragrance, rid my mind of fear with playfulness of her arched eyebrows? When will the auspicious day of love dawn, when my gaze will follow her closely? Will it ever happen,

Fig. 57. The love-lorn lady

Oh my God, that she would pour the perfume of musk and camphor into my heart with her winsome glances? When shall I see her standing like a picture beside the lamp in all her glory and speaking to me smilingly?"

Kṛishṇa's Anxiety (Manifested)

Nāyaka to sakhī: "Ah! If only it could happen that someone suggests to Rādhā's mother to arrange a *svayaṁvara* ceremony for her marriage; her father invites the cow-boys, resembling young gods; she then puts the bridegroom's garland round my neck; and the bride's father gives you away to us as the bride's maid!"

Reminiscence *(Smṛiti)*

Smṛiti Daśā is the state in which nothing else attracts the mind, all business is forgotten, and longing for union is ever-present.

Rādhā's Reminiscence (Secret)

One sakhī to another: "Her anguish has increased so much, that she does not like talk, nor play, nor laugh, nor likes the sight of anything. She does not listen to well-meaning words, nor does she heed them—her mind is so deeply infatuated by someone's love! She looks as if searching within herself for some lost thing, like a person dazed by too much reading and in quest of deep knowledge. Who should devise a diversion for her, or play on the *vīṇā*, for her mind is lost in her own thoughts?"

Fig. 58. Yearnings of love

Rādhā's Reminiscence (Manifested)

Sakhī to nāyikā: "It is no use being so much infatuated by love for him. Your union with him will come about if I will it. You would gain nothing from your continued silence, as that will not bring to you the sweetness of his love. Eschewing both drink and food, how will you live? If the fear of discovery of your present state

Fig. 59. Virahiṇī Nāyikā

does not frighten you, does it not inspire shame in you or arouse your modesty?"

Kṛishṇa's Reminiscence (Secret)

Sakhī to nāyaka: "I smeared your body with camphor-paste mixed with sandal, but that was burnt by its heat and acquired the colour of your skin. Seeing that bower covered with auspicious flowers, your thoughts turned elsewhere. You look as if lost, and move away even though accosted. Your mind is in confusion; I know it is being rocked as if it were in the swing of your beloved's garland."

Kṛishṇa's Reminiscence (Manifested)

One sakhī to another: "Garments and perfumes are like poison to him; the bed bites him like fleas. Sandal and moonlight no longer delight his mind; camphor and the moon torment him. He does not fancy betel-leaves nor likes any drink. All amusements he has abandoned. Which damsel of high caste from Gokula has brought this state upon Kṛishṇa?"

Recalling the Qualities of the Beloved *(Guṇa Kathana)*

Where mental attributes and bodily charm are remembered and described in love's longing, *Guṇa Kathana Daśā* is manifested.

Rādhā's Praise of Kṛishṇa (Secret)

Nāyikā to herself: "The beauty of Kṛishṇa is perfect, while the moon is disfigured by a dark spot. His limbs always look fresh, while the *champaka* leaves fade away if touched. His hands are soft and perfumed, but the lotus-stalk is thorny. His eyes are large and beautiful, but Kāmadeva is blind and his arrows are shot at random!"

Rādhā's Praise of Kṛishṇa (Open)

Nāyikā to sakhī: "What pleases the heart more, the *khañjana* bird or the eyes of my beloved one? Which is sweeter, nectar or his juicy lips? What is more radiant, the pomegranate or his teeth? Which is more pleasant to look at, the moon or his moon-like face? Whose form is more bewitching, Kāmadeva's or his? Which is more soft, the lotus or his lotus-like feet? What is dearer, my life or the picture of my dear one?"

Kṛishṇa's Praise of Rādhā (Secret)

Nāyaka to himself: "I cannot compare her face with the moon, because Rādhā is far more beautiful, nor can I compare it with the lotus because bumble bees harass the lotus. Pomegranate, *śrīphala*, corals, gold (which suffer a thousand indignities by being sold in the market): *chakavā*, pigeon, elephant, snake, tiger, *koel*, parrot (which are impure and filthy) cannot be worthy objects of comparison with her teeth, bosom, lips, complexion, eyes, neck, gait, tresses, waist, voice and nose. Her limbs are, indeed, peerless and their comparison can be only with themselves."

Kṛishṇa's Praise of Rādhā (Open)

Nāyaka to sakhī: "Rādhā's beauty has bewitched my eyes. Decorated with thick saffron paste, she is as if engulfed with my love. The colour of my skin has as if been transferred

Fig. 60. Lady in distress

to her blue garments. Smelling a lotus, she stands yonder, as if inhaling the fragrance (love) of my heart."

Agitation *(Udvega)*

Udvega Daśā is that state wherein things, which normally give delight, begin to cause pain.

Rādhā's Agitation (Secret)

Nāyikā to herself: "This moon is in fact the source of poison; that is why Rāhu could not devour it all at once, and the holy Agastya having swallowed it while drinking up the ocean, could not digest it. Brahmā, the Creator, foolishly gave the name of *sudhādhara* (one who possesses nectar) to the moon, and of *vishadhara* (one who possesses poison) to Śeshanāga. What shall one say of the sun who has given it a position of equal importance (by sharing its light with it)?"

Rādhā's Agitation (Manifested)

Sakhī to nāyaka: "Yesterday, on seeing you, she ran away out of bashfulness; today she is on the verge of dying, not being able to see you. During day time, she is as if submerged in poison; at night she burns in moonlight. She shifts from the bed to the ground and from the ground back to the bed in the agony of love. You may send an ornament from your body, seeing which she may have some relief."

Kṛishṇa's Agitation (Secret)

Sakhī to nāyikā: "He is as indifferent to the swans, as the clouds are to them; he heeds not the clouds, as the swans do not care to drink water from them. He does not delight in the sight of the moon even as the lotuses do not; he does not care to touch lotus flowers just as the moon avoids touching them. He no longer takes his usual stroll between the pool and the garden, nor does he frequent the lovers' tryst where *tāla* and *tamāla* trees grow. How strange are those girls who, hearing of such a condition of their beloved ones, can manage to live even for a moment!"

Kṛishṇa's Agitation (Manifested)

Sakhī to nāyikā: "His eyes brim with tears in remembrance of you; seeing the *tamāla* trees his whole body shivers. He wanders in silence, sometimes to your garden and sometimes to the pool as if he has lost his way. If you wish to see him, why don't you go? I would not go with you to show him in this condition. Only now have you felt the desire to see him, when nothing pleases him."

Delirium *(Pralāpa)*

Pralāpa Daśā is created when the lover's mind wanders like a bumble bee, and, along with the body, suffers intense torment, and when the lover talks always of the beloved one.

Nāyikā's Delirium (Secret)

One sakhī to another describing nāyikā's condition: "Her eyes are brimming again and again with tears. She complained of Kṛishṇa's harsh words saying that they had added to her

Fig. 61. The love-lorn lady

Fig. 62. The utter desolation of virahiṇī

Fig. 63. 'Give me the news of my dear one, Oh cloud!'

Fig. 64. Thoughts of the lover

pain. Now there is no playfulness for her, nor laughter, frolic, friendliness, or enmity. She has as if no dealings with anyone, nor relationship, nor even a nodding acquaintance."

Nāyikā's Delirium (Manifested)

Nāyikā to sakhī: "While I was playing with my friends, Kṛishṇa approached secretly from behind. I did not see him, when the immodest one held me from the back. I was stricken with shame, my heart burned with such anger as I have never felt before. I suffer this anguish on account of (the folly of) my eyes."

Kṛishṇa's Delirium (Secret)

One sakhī to another: "Struck by her beauty, Kṛishṇa persistently questioned me on oath about her : Who was she that hid her face in her blue garment, and, leaning on the door, concealed herself behind you, and later having seen me ran inside and was heard talking laughingly from within?"

Kṛishṇa's Delirium (Manifested)

Nāyaka to sakhī: "Who is she and on what purpose has she come to your house, treading on the lotuses of her admirers' eyes; whose winsome laughter is like sunshine; whose fragrance is like camphor; whose dark tresses plaited with white pearls and red thread, look like the confluence of three rivers, the white Gaṅgā, the dark Yamunā and the red Sarasvatī, in which my longings like hermits take the holy dip; whose eyes look charmed by someone's love and desirous of seeing their object of love; whose eyebrows are beautifully arched, and budding breasts stand on tiptoe?"

Frenzy *(Unmāda Daśā)*

Unmāda Daśā (frenzy) is that in which the lover sits engrossed in thought, then rises and walks away, keeps staring at the beloved one's face and weeps and laughs profusely.

Rādhā's Frenzy (Secret)

Sakhī to nāyaka: "Her anguish has so increased in your separation that she has lost her wits. Her hairs are dishevelled and are dangling in confusion on her back. With difficulty can she manage to stand or look round. She sinks into thoughts on seeing others, and burns all the more from remedies adopted to relieve her love anguish. Breathing heavily, she is as if without consciousness; it appears as though she has been caught by the demon of love."

Rādhā's Frenzy (Manifested)

Sakhī to nāyaka: "She stares as if startled; her heart beats heavily and seeing her own shadow she loses herself in thought. Her answers are irrelevant to the questions asked of her; in separation she has become an altogether changed person. Someone's evil eye has caught her, or a touch of insanity has affected her, or an evil spell has been cast on her. Thus deranged, she is now indifferent to her veil, her garments and her ornaments."

Kṛishṇa's Frenzy (Secret)

One sakhī to another: "Sometimes he talks subtly and sometimes casually, sometimes of mundane and sometimes of metaphysical matters. Sometimes he weeps and sometimes

Fig. 65. Grief on separation from the lover

Fig. 66. Lady in distress

Fig. 67. Remembrance of past union

Fig. 68. Lady in swoon

sings and dances immodestly. His mind has lost its balance, and his body is without any animation. Has he been affected by a woman's love, or a touch of insanity, or has some evil one deprived him of his wits?"

Kṛishṇa's Frenzy (Manifested)

Sakhī to Rādhā: "With tearful eyes and dazed mind he gazes all around, then stares fixedly, and then walks away hurriedly. He keeps brooding with agitated mind and fever in his body. Sometimes he weeps and sometimes laughs. Fear-stricken and agitated in my mind, I have come to tell you of his condition. He is talking so incoherently that I fear lest the secret of his love for you may not be disclosed."

Sickness *(Vyādhi)*

Vyādhi Daśā is that in which the colour of the body assumes pallor, breathing becomes heavy, eyes shed profuse tears and the mind's anguish is very great (Fig. 68).

Rādhā's Sickness (Secret)

Sakhī to nāyikā: "He has given up his flute and here you have been struck dumb. Neither

Fig. 69. Detail of Fig. 68

Fig. 70. Rādhā in swoon — Illustration to the Karuṇā-bharaṇa

of you hears nor understands anything when spoken to. He does not eat the betel-leaf, and you have given up even water. Is it the effect of love, or of an evil spirit, for you are constantly raving about each other? Such a situation would shake anyone's wisdom. Have you outwitted him or has he outwitted you?"

Kṛishṇa's Sickness (Manifested)

One sakhī to another: "There his body burns with fever, nor do the remedies adopted to relieve her of anguish prove any good. There, his heavy breathing as if makes you fly, and here her profuse weeping gives you a bath of tears. The mystery of the love of Kṛishṇa and Rādhā is not understood, for something has happened to them both at the same time."

In *vyādhi* the body is wasted by the fever of love. There is a very touching picture of this stage of love in a series illustrating the drama *Karuṇā-bharaṇa* by the artist of the *Bhāgavata Purāṇa* series in which Kṛishṇa is shown on a visit to Kurukshetra on the occasion of a solar eclipse and is meeting Nanda and Yaśodā in their camp. After embracing Nanda he is proceeding towards Yaśodā, and Rādhā, who has learnt the news of his arrival, faints. *Gopīs* are bowing in deep veneration, and even the cows and calves are greeting Kṛishṇa with their faces uplifted. Rādhā who has fainted is shown in a corner being attended by the other *gopīs* (Figs. 70 and 71).

Stupor *(Jaḍatā)*

Jaḍatā Daśā (stupor) is that state in which all consciousness is lost and the sensation given by pleasure and pain is the same.

Rādhā's Stupor (Secret)

One sakhī to another: "Suitable remedies have a cooling effect on feverish bodies, but here, in spite of such remedies, her body is pining away. Any other remedy may worsen her condition. You can see how she is fading away! What shall we do then? To whom shall we go? How shall she live, and how shall we live without her?"

Rādhā's Stupor (Manifested)

Sakhī to nāyaka: "First she met you in person, then through the help of her friends, then through the medium of letters. Finding this dissatisfying, she met you in her imagination, as a poor person dreams of gold. You should now go and meet her, lest the inevitable should befall her; for if in the supreme contemplation of love, she is united to her lord, all distance between you and her will be removed."

Kṛishṇa's Stupor (Secret)

One sakhī to another: "His body is getting colder and colder; all remedies have been thought of and tried. Whatever you may do to his body it gives him no sensation of pleasure or pain. He hears and understands nothing. Whom shall we consult now; who shall know his disease now? No one knows if this is the result of *yoga* or the outcome of separation."

Fig. 71. Detail of Fig. 70

Kṛishṇa's Stupor (Manifested)

Sakhī to nāyikā: "He has cast his garments away; he lives on air and has withdrawn his senses from external objects and his mind is as if in supreme contemplation *(samādhi)*. Do not malign him but wait till he wins glory through his penance, which he is doing for your sake, O lady! If you cannot grant boons, you can at least give him the gift of life."

Death of Lovers *(Maraṇa Daśā)*

Maraṇa Daśā occurs in the fullness of love, when separation from the beloved one continues and union is not brought about with guile or force.

CHAPTER IX

LOVE IN UNION

Saṁyoga

When two lovers, mutually enamoured, are engaged in looking at each other, or touching each other, it is called 'Love in Union' *(Saṁyoga* or *Saṁbhoga)*. There are numerous illustrations of phases of love in union, ranging from lovers seated together to love scenes of utmost intimacy. Such love scenes are seen in illustrations of the *Gīta Govinda*, the *Rasikapriyā*, the *Satsaiyyā*, the romance of Nala-Damayantī, as well as in the Śiva-Pārvatī paintings. Plates XVI to XX illustrate various themes relating to love in union. Very beautiful are these love scenes with the lovers happy together; the piquant upturn of the lady's face as she looks at her lover, who in turn glances at her with tender affection. These happy couples, intensely interested in one another and admiring each other with such warmth are eloquent symbols of love, that noble emotion which uplifts humanity from the animal level, and in whose glow we see the

Fig. 72. Kṛishṇa combing Rādhā's hair

Fig. 73. Hari and Rādhā are making obeisance to spring

Fig. 74. Sheltering from rain

Fig. 75. Joy of being together

Fig. 76. How delightful the clouds!

Fig. 77. Admiring the flight of cranes

Fig. 78. Rādhā and Kṛishṇa on a swing

Fig. 79. The couch of love

birth of true poetry, painting as well as religion. Like the Japanese artists of the Tokugawa regime, the Vaishṇava mystics did not distinguish between sensuousness and spirituality. One leads into the other, and we see at once the spiritual in the sensuous.

The divine love of Rādhā and Kṛishṇa is depicted in a painting from Guler, where they are shown seated on a lotus as Vishṇu and Lakshmī. Kṛishṇa holding a flute is looking at Rādhā with longing. His plume of peacock feathers, his garland of wild flowers, and the hem of his yellow *pītāmbara* are fluttering in the air. His beauty, like the radiance of the full moon, illumines the bank of the lotus-studded lake. On the bank are adoring groups of cow-girls and cow-boys with their offerings. The picture is suffused with love, and is an excellent example of love in union (Fig. 1).

In Fig. 72 Kṛishṇa is combing Rādhā's hair, and she is looking at his face reflected in the mirror of the ring *(ārasī)* on her finger, for she does not want to lose sight of the face of her lover even for a moment. Combing of each other's hair is a favourite love-play in India. The pigeons on the shades of windows, and pointed cypresses among the globose crowns of mangoes provide an appropriate atmosphere for this interesting painting showing love in union.

A delightful painting depicting love in union in spring shows a tryst by the river bank. In a shady nook is a bed of leaves covered with jasmines. The stream that winds along the bower, courts the shore with waves of love. Flowering creepers are clinging passionately to the trunks of trees, and sprays of blossoms are dangling in the air. On the branches of the trees are pairs of love-birds. Kṛishṇa's bright yellow clothes are like lightnings flashing on the body, which is blue like a mass of water-laden clouds. The peacock feathers crowning his head put the colours of the rainbow to shame. His eyes are like two pure lotus petals, and on his forehead is the mark of sandal-paste. Here two hearts are beating in unison, and this is the course of love. In the enchanting lovers' nest Hari and Rādhā are making obeisance to the auspicious *Vasanta* (Spring) (Fig. 73).

The following poem is inscribed on the painting:

> In a beautiful bower laden with flowers on the bank of Kālindī
> Resounding with joyful cries of peacocks
> And the pleasing rumble of water-laden clouds
> Kṛishṇa kisses the sweet lips of Rādhā.
> All homage to the Gardener of the Forest
> The Flute Player Divine!

Love-birds sitting in pairs, creepers clasping the trees, the swirling current of the river hugging the bank are the poetic symbols by which the artist creates an atmosphere of love, and how effectively he uses them in the painting!

Paintings illustrating love in union during the rains are numerous. The onset of the monsoon with dark rolling clouds, the play of lightning, the flight of egrets and *sāras* cranes against slate blue clouds, and the shouting of peacocks have a strange fascination for the Indian mind. The Hindi poets have sung of the joy of rains, and the Kangra artists have given expression to that joy in their paintings. The frontispiece, Plates XVI, XVII and XVIII, and Figs. 74–77 illustrate the joy of rains. How tender, soft, warm in tone and atmosphere are these paintings! Here are forms which are poems, and colours that are melodies. The most delicate and poetic of these is the painting from Guler given as frontispiece. The sinuous flashes of lightning in the dark clouds, the white cranes and music create a mood of joy which we can sense in the faces of the lovers. Cattle grazing on the village common, villagers crossing the river on inflated skins, water-mills in a corner, and hamlets concealed among bamboos, mangoes and plantains remind us of the lower hills of the Kangra Valley. Mystical affinity between the life of Nature and the life of man, between the beauty of love, and the beauty of clouds and flying birds finds eloquent expression in this painting. Plate XVII and Fig. 74 represent the same theme, viz. Rādhā and Kṛishṇa sheltering from rain under a dark blanket. Here the sudden onset of rain has provided a pretext to the lovers for being together. A pair of cow-boys hiding in the hollow bole of a tree, cow-girls hurrying towards the village, and cranes flying away in panic indicate the intensity of the storm.

Fig. 76 is a delightful drawing showing lovers' happiness on the advent of rains. An atmosphere is created by the activity which is going on in the rooms below the pavilion: a lady is decorating her forehead; and another one is emptying stale water from a flask. On the shade above the window is a restless peacock, about to fly away. His mate is shouting on the roof of the pavilion. On the edge of the bed is lying a flower-garland. The lovers are admiring the flight of cranes in the dark rolling clouds. There is a feeling of joy on the face of the lady. The Hindus, like the Japanese, are lovers of the moon. They compare the beautiful face of a woman to the moon. On moonlit nights lovers go out in search of each other. Special festivals are celebrated on the night of the full moon in each month, and moon-viewing is a favourite pastime. Like the Japanese, they also admire the friendly light of the moon filtering through the crowns of trees. The special favourites of the ancient Hindus were Moonlight Gardens with dark trees and fragrant white flowers like *champaka*, *mogrā*, gardenias and jasmines. They admired the sweet solitude of these gardens, filled with the fragrance of flowers, which floats in the air like an invisible dryad, and intoxicates the senses. The most delightful paintings of lovers admiring the moon are in the '*Nala-Damayantī Drawings*' recently published by Eastman, in some of which the lovers are shown rapturously hailing the moon rising over the mountains. Kangra paintings of love in moonlight reproduced here are Plates VIII and XIX, and Fig. 79. In Fig. 79 the lovers are seated on a bed of leaves, the couch of love. The half moon in the sky has spread charm over the landscape. The dark trees are tenderly clasped by the *mādhavī* creeper, and its blossoms are gently swaying over the lovers. On the lovely face of the lady is the glow of hundred flowers in bloom. There is love in her eyes, and joy in her heart.

CHAPTER X

THE TWELVE MONTHS

Bārāmāsā

The pageant of the seasons, with the warmth of spring following the cold of winter, and the heat of summer fading into the chill of autumn with its russet tints has delighted mankind for ages. Representations of the seasons and months are frequent themes in the classical and medieval art of the West. "In the archaic and classical art of Greece, the Seasons are usually shown in full figures and participate in some mythological scene; in early Roman art they appear as isolated figures and in late Roman art as isolated busts."[20] Early representations of the seasons were all female. Male representations developed in the 2nd century A.D. and were most frequently reproduced in the 3rd century, especially on coins, sarcophagi and mosaics. Then developed pictorial rustic calendars showing agricultural, civil and religious activities. In the 4th century A.D. developed the 'active' season with one or more figures engaged on work associated with the season. Another manner of depicting the seasons was to place them in the four corners of concentric images of the universe as in Hrabanus Maurusas De Universe, a codex written at Monte Cassino in Italy in A.D. 1023. In Tacuinum pictures of the seasons from Italy, spring is shown as women picking flowers and making wreaths, summer by reaping corn, autumn by a vintage scene, and winter as an old man warming himself at an open fire. The number of pictorial representations of the 'Labours of the Months' in the Middle Ages of Europe is very great, and a fixed iconography was evolved for each month. From the 14th to 16th centuries, a number of miniatures depicting the twelve months were produced in France.

Rice has shown that in the 13th and 14th centuries, the representation of the seasons and months was borrowed from Western models in Islamic art. He has described a manuscript from the Bodleian Library, Oxford, known as the *Kitāb al-bulhān* (Book of Well-being) illustrated by one Abdal Hassan, a native of Baghdad attributed to A.D. 1399, in which apart from instructions on food, medicines, baths, and frequency of sexual intercourse, there are illustrations of the seasons, represented in the following manner:

Spring: A youth in an orange robe and white turban seated under a tree playing a flute. In the centre of the picture is a peach tree in bloom.

Summer: A young man in a pale orange robe stepping forward to draw a bow, and aiming at a flying bird. In the top right corner is the hot sun with golden rays. Fruit-bearing orange and apple trees are also depicted.

Autumn: A youth in a pale robe holding a gold cup filled with wine kneels in the centre of the picture. Trees have rust-red leaves.

Winter: An indoor scene, a man sitting in a bed propped against an orange cushion warming his hands over a brazier.

There is a mood of sadness about Autumn and joyfulness in the Spring and Summer pictures.

It is doubtful if the Islamic paintings of the 14th century from Baghdad had any influence on Indian painting. The earliest known Indian paintings of the months included in the set of illustrations of the love legend of *Laur-Chandā* are from Central India. These are in the Punjab Museum, Patiala, and in the Central Museum, Lahore. They closely resemble the *Chaurapañchāśikā* series of paintings which Archer has ascribed to the Mandu-Malwa School and has dated A.D. 1550. They, however, bear no resemblance to the paintings from Baghdad.

THE SIX SEASONS

The earliest account of the seasons in Sanskrit literature is found in the *Ṛitusaṁhāra* of the poet Kālidāsa, a poem written in six cantos answering to the six Indian seasons, Summer, Rain, Autumn, Early Winter, Winter and Spring. It is not merely a description of the seasons, but is much more an account of the feelings awakened by the changing seasons in lovers, given in a warm sensuous style in rich harmonious splendour of sound and language. He gives vivid descriptions of beauty in Nature, of mango trees in bloom, the charming *palāśas* appearing like lighted torches, the fragrance of the *ketakī* in the rains, the warm southern wind, the murmur of wild bees, the distant cry of the demoiselle crane, the love-calls of the *koel* in mango groves, the fields of paddy with their fringes adorned by herds of deer, the loveliness of lakes and rivers, the wild beauty of the forests, and the grandeur of the mountains. His voluptuous descriptions of the reactions of the lovers to the changing scenery are suffused with love. During the heat of the summer, women with rounded hips, whose grace is enhanced by soft white silk, and breasts cooled by the fragrant sandal-paste, soothe the senses of their lovers. In the rainy season women with long glossy black hair reaching their hips, with ears decorated with fragrant blossoms, and lips moist with wine, fill their lovers' mind with longing. In autumn the beams of the moon burn the delicate limbs of the lovely maiden pining in separation from her lover. In early winter the young lovers, their mouths fragrant with the perfume of wine, sleep twined in each other's arms steeped in the luscious flavour of love. In the long winter nights the young lovers are ruthless in the sports of love, and late in the night the young wives with tired limbs tread their way to their rooms. In the morning the youthful wife, with a lovely slender waist, deep navel, and ample hips is about to leave the bed and is loosely binding her hair in which the chaplet of flowers is fading. In spring, the young women are attuned to love's instinct, yawning, their limbs relax, and their bodies, dissolving in amorous languor, snuggle, beside their lovers. Seeing the mango trees in bloom, the passer-by away from his beloved feels the pangs of separation and sobs.

BĀRĀMĀSĀ

Bārāmāsā has been the favourite theme in religious and secular poetry of the Punjab and in the ballads of East Bengal.[21] The earliest *Bārāmāsā* is by Guru Nanak (1469-1538) in which there are vivid descriptions of the beauty of Nature apart from remembrance of God. Guru Arjan's (1581-1606) *Bārāmāsā* in the *Guru Granth* is remarkable for its mystic flavour. In the poetry of Bulheshah (A.D. 1680-1752), the well-known Sufi mystic poet, there are interesting descriptions of the months. In Punjabi folk-song also *Bārāmāsā* is a favourite theme.

The twelve months of the year, *Bārāmāsā*, provided a delightful theme to the Hindi poets, and their descriptions are still read with joy. An account of the twelve months is given by Keshav Dās in the tenth chapter of the *Kavipriyā*, and he describes the life of the people in different seasons, their ceremonies and rituals. In describing how the *nāyikā* should prevail upon the *nāyaka* not to leave her and proceed on a journey, he gives an account of the months, mentioning the delights of the Spring months, *Chaitra* and *Baisākha*, the heat of *Jyeshṭha* and *Āshāḍha*, the showers of *Śrāvaṇa* and *Bhādon*, *Āśvina* when the sky is clear, the bright *Kārttika*, the pleasant *Agahana* when demoiselle cranes shout joyfully, the chilly *Pausha*, the pleasant *Māgha* when the four quarters are perfumed with sandal and camphor, and the delightful *Phālguna*, the month of love. *Bārāmāsā* has been a favourite theme with the Pahari painters. The Kangra painters have rendered in colour and line the word pictures of Keshav Dās. There is a set of twelve paintings, dating from the reign of Maharaja Sansar Chand, in the collection of the Raja of Lambagraon in which the *Bārāmāsā* of Keshav Dās is illustrated.[22] They do not bear the name of any artist. Out of these, Plates XXI, XXII and XXIV have been reproduced in this book. Plate XXI illustrates the spring month of *Chaitra*, Plate XXII, the month of *Śrāvaṇa*, Plate XXIII, the month of *Bhādon* and Plate XXIV, the month of *Agahana*. The landscape and buildings shown in these paintings remind us of the towns of Tira-Sujanpur, Alampur and the countryside along the river Beas. These paintings may be dated *c.* 1790, the period when Sansar Chand was at the peak of his glory. In these paintings we have a graphic account of the twelve months of the year. In each, a human couple in the form of Rādhā and Kṛishṇa is shown in the foreground, their dresses varying according to the month. The landscape in the background illustrates the vegetation, and the reactions of animal and human life to the changes in temperature. A similar set of drawings is in the collection of the Bhārat Kalā Bhavan, Varanasi. The iconography of Kangra *Bārāmāsā* paintings is more or less faithfully copied in another set of paintings in an inferior style in the collection of the Raja of Suket, which were possibly painted at Suket about 1830. Plate XXV, illustrating the month of *Pausha* (December), is from another set of twelve paintings possibly executed by a Guler artist for a Sikh patron.

There is a set of *Bārāmāsā* paintings in the Bhuri Singh Museum, Chamba, painted during the rule of Raja Charat Singh about 1830. There is another series in the Kasturbhai Lalbhai collection, Ahmedabad, possibly painted at Sibā during the rule of Raja Gobind Singh (*c.* 1820-30), in which two fortresses are seen on both sides of a river, very reminiscent of the fortresses of Dādā and Sibā on the Beas. There is a painting of the month of *Āsoja* which bears an inscription from the *Kavipriyā* and also the signatures of the artist Chhajū (Fig. 84). Chhajū was the grandson of Nainsukh, and son of Kāmā, the artist who it seems migrated from Kangra to Chamba. Paintings of *Māgha* and *Kārttika* in the collection of the Bhārat Kalā Bhavan, Varanasi, are in the same style and are the work of Chhajū.

In the Sanskrit and Hindi literature of "The Twelve Months", we find complete harmony of man and his environment. There is no grumbling against the elements, and no complaints against the weather. Each season is to be enjoyed. When it is hot, the joy of wearing light muslin clothes and bathing in cold water compensate for the heat. When it is cold, the lovers enjoy the pleasure of snuggling in warm blankets and sitting near the fire-side (Plate XXV). It is, however, the spring and the rains which are the real seasons of love in Northern India.

The emotions of lovers are eloquently portrayed in the paintings in which the poetry is given visual form.

The recurring theme of the *Bārāmāsā* poems is that of love in union, or of love in separation. The lovers who are together are happy, while those who are separated on account of travel or otherwise suffer the torment of separation. In paintings where a human couple is shown, the prevailing sentiment is that of love in union. Standing on terraces, admiring clouds and lightning or snuggling in pavilions in gardens, they proclaim the joys of *saṁyoga* (love in union). The cooling showers of rain, the sailing clouds, the play of lightning in the clouds, the rainbow decorating the sky, and the autumn moon, all these are excitants of love. To the woman who is separated from her lover, these are no more pleasing; the moon beams burn her body, and even the rain showers give her no comfort.

Now let us follow the caravan of the seasons through the twelve months of the year in Northern India. The Hindu year is divided into six seasons, each season consisting of two months. Summer scorches the countryside in the months of May and June. Then follow the rains from July to middle of September. When the skies have cleared in the month of October, autumn, with its beautiful cloud-effects and golden sunsets begins, and the nights sparkle with moonlight. From November to the first half of December is the early winter, the *Hemanta*, when the climate becomes cool and bracing. From the latter half of December to early February is the winter, the *Śiśira*, when there is biting cold, fields are covered with frost, and snow falls in the Himalayas. *Vasanta*, the spring, comprises the months of March and first half of April. According to prevailing temperature, the year can be divided into four seasons, spring, summer, autumn and winter, which can be compared to the four parts of the day, the dawn, noon, sunset, and the night. Spring corresponds to the dawn, summer to the noon, autumn to sunset, and winter to the night. They also correspond to the four stages in the life of man, childhood, youth, middle age and old age.

The description of the months given by Keshav Dās apply to Northern India, where there is severe cold in winter which contrasts with the heat of summer, and not to Southern India, which has a tropical climate. In some cases the descriptions of the months are poetic idealization of these times of year rather than realistic or factual accounts.

Chaitra

The month of *Chaitra* is heralded by the cooing of doves and the yellow flowers of *sarson*, which wave like a sea of gold. The *śīśam* trees get covered with pale green silk-like leaves. Men and women wear saffron clothes and harmonize with Nature.

The lover and his beloved are seated on a terrace with the background of flowering shrubs in which birds of many kinds are warbling music. The lady is asking her lover not to go on travels in the month of *Chaitra* (Plate XXI). The month of *Chaitra* is thus described by Keshav Dās:

> Lovely creepers are in bloom,
> blossoming trees are young once more,
> And streams and lakes are full of flowers.
> Women, aglow with passion
> and dressed in their best,
> Abandon themselves to sports of love.
> The parrot, the *mainā* and the *koel*
> are singing songs of love.
> Why think of going away, why spoil this joy
> in the month of *Chaitra*, my love?

Baisākha

In the month of *Baisākha* trees produce new leaves, *pīpal* trees get covered with coppery leaves, and appear most charming. When the slanting rays of the evening sun strike the young leaves of the *pīpal*, they appear like a cloud of fire. In damp places myriads of fire-flies are seen twinkling like stars, and weaving aerial dances in fragile rhythms of flickering gold. Dry leaves of trees fly about, and weird bonfires are seen under *mahuā* trees. The air is heavy with the fragrance of *nim* and *śirīsha* flowers, and the quiet of the night is disturbed by the rattling noise of *śirīsha* pods. The rust-red young leaves of *mahuās* are tipped with gold in the rays of the morning sun. *Gul mohurs* are flushing into vivid scarlet, and it is getting warm.

The *kachnār* trees, which in winter appeared so unattractive with leafless branches, produce a rich harvest of pink, white and purple-mauve blossoms and for full one month add colour and charm to the landscape. The delicate blossoms of *kachnār* trees fill one's heart with bliss and soothe the eyes. Then follows the *semal*, the silk-cotton tree. The gaunt limbs of the *semal* are decorated with cup-like scarlet flowers, and the tree reminds one of the goddess Lakshmī, with numerous arms, holding scarlet lamps in the palms of her outstretched hands.[23] The sombre mango groves suddenly begin to pulsate with life, and produce pale yellow blossoms in profusion. These are the sharp arrows with which the god of love enflames the hearts of maidens to love. Attracted by the fragrance of mango blossoms *koels* come to the mango gardens, which are filled with the pleasant echoes of their calls. By the middle of *Baisākha*, Spring is in its prime. Who is not filled with yearning thoughts of love when the air swoons with the scent of mango blossoms, and is filled with the hum of bees intoxicated with honey.

The *nāyaka* and *nāyikā* are seated on a terrace against the background of a hill. Near by is a hamlet, and farmers are busy harvesting wheat (Fig. 80). The painting illustrates the following poem of Keshav Dās:

The earth and heavens are full of fragrance;
The scented breeze blows softly,
  laden with the nectar of flowers.
There is beauty everywhere,
  Sweet perfume fills the air.
This erotic fragrance, this season of wistful love
  has maddened the sporting bees
And fills the forlorn heart
  with longings for the home,
I pray thee who has made me so happy
  to abide here, this month of *Baisākha*.
For I know from experience, my love!
In separation the shafts of *Kāma* are hard to bear.

Jyeshṭha

The hot sun scorches the landscape. The sky is coppery, and the air is full of dust. Peacocks sit like statues amidst the trees and pray for rain. Oblivious of the presence of peahens, who follow them in the shade of the trees, they hide their burning heads below their tails. The hot dry wind blowing over sand-dunes produces mirages of rivers and lakes attracting herds of deer for miles. Even tigers are fatigued and lie languidly in their caves. The whole firmament is aglow with the dazzling radiation of the sun. The lakes which were filled with pink and white lotuses a month ago are drying. Thirsty buffaloes are wallowing in mud with their tongues protruding. Forest fires cause havoc among the denizens of the forest. Oppressed by heat elephants rend the air with their trumpeting, and cobras leave their holes. Wayfarers seek the hospitable shade of mango groves, and quench their thirst from the *piayo*. The lovely lady draped in blue stands on the terrace, with palms of her hands dyed red with henna, conversing with her lover, prevailing upon him not to leave her. The golden yellow racemes of *amaltās* provide a delightful contrast with the blue drapery of the lady (Fig. 81). Keshav Dās thus describes the hot month of *Jyeshṭha:*

Air, Water, Sky, Earth and Fire
These elements become one, a burning fire.
Weary feels the wayfarer,
  and tame is the wild elephant
  seeing the dried up pond.

Fig. 80. The month of Baisākha

Fig. 81. The month of Jyeshṭha

The cobra nestles in his trunk,
  and the tiger slumbers in his shade.
All creatures of earth and water
  are feeble and know no rest.
That is why the wise enjoin,
  do not leave home in *Jyeshṭha*.

Āshāḍha

Hot winds blow and scorch the vegetation. Dust devils are seen whirling into brown spirals linking the earth with the heavens, and sucking leaves and dust into their bodies. The fierce rays of the sun beat mercilessly on the coppery earth, and the atmosphere is filled with stifling dust. All the men, birds, and beasts seek shelter in shade. Even the wandering ascetics give up their travels. The lady wearing a transparent muslin *dupaṭṭā*, the palms of her hands dyed with henna, is imploring her lover not to leave her alone in such a hot month. In the foreground is a fountain shooting up jets of water, and in the background is a temple with a group of ascetics resting, while a man is pulling water out of a well (Fig. 82). The painting illustrates the following poem of Keshav Dās:

Fig. 82. The month of Āshāḍha

Fig. 83. The month of Bhādon

Faster and faster the whirlwinds blow,
like the crazy thoughts of one away from home.
The wandering ascetics move out no more,
The birds would not leave their nests,
and Nārāyaṇa and Lakshmī, too, have gone to rest.
Why think of going, my love,
when none in *Āshāḍha* leaves his home?

Śrāvaṇa

After the parching heat of June, clouds appear in the sky, and provide joy to the farmers anxiously waiting for the rain, as well as to the lovers in search of coolness. Like a mighty army the clouds march with drum-like thundering. On the sight of the purple clouds and on hearing the sound of thunder, peacocks shout with joy, and spread their rainbow-coloured tail-feathers into gorgeous fans. Life wakes and shines, and the forest seems to show its glee in flowering *kadambas* which are covered with yellow ball-like flowers. The opening sheath of *ketakī* blossom is like a smile put on to greet the reviving breath of rain. The graceful creepers vie with the arms of lovely women.

Fig. 84. The month of Āsoja (Āśvina)

Fig. 85. The month of Āśvina

Rain-clouds drench the earth and the thirsty brown earth suddenly gets covered with a carpet of green grass. Velvet mites, the scarlet *birbahutis*, and brides of the heroes, make the earth look like a pretty woman decked with sparkling gems. The rain patters on the leaves of the mangoes, and exquisite music flows from the crowns of the mango trees. Crowds of children and women wander in the groves in search of ripe-golden mangoes filled with nectar-like juice, which drop from the branches. Rice fields shine like mirrors. The rain-drops give birth to iridescent bubbles on the placid waters of the village pond, which, after their momentary glamour, merge into the water of the pond. On the leaves of the lotuses tremulous pearls of water dance restlessly.

The sound of the approaching rain-shower and the sight of the rolling clouds fill the hearts of lovers with bliss. Rain-charged clouds bend down to kiss the towering rocks, and streams gush down their slopes. Throngs of peacocks begin to dance with joy. The lovers seated on a *chaukī* on a terrace are watching the play of lightning (Plate XXII).

The painting illustrates the following poem of Keshav Dās on the month of *Śrāvaṇa:*

> The streams look so lovely,
>   as they rush to meet the sea.
> The creepers enchant the eye,
>   embracing young trees lovingly.

Fig. 86. The month of Kārttika

Fig. 87. The month of Pausha

The lightning flashes restlessly,
as she sports with rolling clouds.
The peacocks with their shrill cries
announce the mating of earth and sky.
All lovers meet in this month of *Śrāvaṇa*,
why forsake me then, my love?

Bhādon

Clouds rumble ceaselessly, and in the dark night water drips continuously from the leaves of trees and creepers shaken by the powerful wind. The bees have forgotten all about honey and the fragrance of flowers, and are hiding themselves in heaps. Rivers are swollen with turbid water, in whose mighty current large trees uprooted from the banks are tossed about like straw.

Bhādon is the month of lovers, amorous and passionate. In the cool and fragrant breeze of *Bhādon*, lovers who are parted, feel unhappy and long for each other. Brides away from their husbands feel sad. Lovers who are united watch the dark rolling clouds and the flashes of lightning. On hearing the deafening peals of thunder, the amorous lady was startled,

Fig. 88. The month of Māgha

Fig. 89. The month of Phālguna

and embraced her lover. Cleaving the dark clouds with their golden legs are flights of white cranes who provide a thrill to the lovers drunk with joy of the rainy season (frontispiece). What Laurence Binyon says about a similar Kangra drawing very aptly applies here: "The gesture of the lovers as they watch the flight of herons over the lake, the movement of the attendant maids who play music to them — every form and movement in the design melts naturally into the spontaneous rhythm that controls the whole. You feel the artist's joy in the tracing of his lines just for their own sake; yet this is fused with the joy that overflows and radiates from the whole design. Many a Western artist would try to express that joy merely through the faces of lovers. Here every line is eloquent! Is there anything in the art of the world so like a song that sings itself?"[24]

The moist air of *Bhādon* is drenched with the fragrance of jasmines, and the Queen of the Night, and *mehndi* exhales delicate fragrance. The white flowers of gardenia are studded over the hedges like stars in the dark blue sky. The golden glowing *champaka* buds are pouring their fragrance in the air. Women decorate their tress-knots with the white *champaka*, "the moon hanging by the mountain", and wear bracelets of jasmine round their wrists.

The lady standing on a terrace is pointing towards the falling rain and is imploring her lover to stay with her in the delightful month of *Bhādon* (Fig. 83). This painting illustrates the following poem of Keshav Dās:

> The purple clouds are gathering, the thunder rolls
> and rain pours in torrents.
> The wind blows fiercely, the cicadas chirp,
> the lions roar, and elephants fell the trees.
> The day is dark like the night,
> and one's own home is the best.
> Pray leave me not in the month of *Bhādon*,
> for separation pains like poison.

Āśvina (Āsoja)

The rains have ended. The atmosphere is freed of dust and haze, the sky is deep blue, and the air is cool in *Āśvina.* The autumn has come beauteous as a newly-wedded bride, with face of full-blown lotuses and robe of ripening paddy. The wind comes trembling through the burdened paddy-stalks, making a flowery ripple of the lotus-covered lake. White blossoms of silver grass wave gracefully in the air along the banks of rivers. In the blue sky float pure white rainless cumulus clouds, like cotton-wool scattered by the bow of a wool carder. Glorious sunsets are seen, and the earth appears like a fairy wrapped in pink and russet drapery. The autumn-flowering *kachnār* and the *kovidāra* trees, are laden with thousands of pink purple flowers which invite myriads of bees. The white blossoms of jasmine showing through the garniture of dark green leaves, rival the dazzling teeth of smiling maidens.

In the Kangra Valley the *padam,* the carmine cherry, is a never-to-be-forgotten sight. The *padam* with its carmine blossoms dangling in clusters, seen against the blue Himalayan sky, lighted by the rays of the setting sun, appears like a cloud of fire. "I am the rose-cloud of pleasure floating in the dream of the Autumn", says the *padam.* The leaves of the oaks are rich brown, and the maples and chestnuts with their golden-brown leaves stand out conspicuously among the other trees of the forest.

Āśvina is the month of religious ceremonies, when the spirits of the departed ancestors are propitiated. The *nāyaka* is consoling the *nāyikā* who is feeling sad at the thought of his impending departure on travels. In the background are a lotus lake and a temple. The buildings on the hillock to the left are very reminiscent of Tira-Sujanpur (Fig. 85). In a painting of *Āsoja* from Chamba by the artist Chhajū, Brahmin priests are shown worshipping in front of a temple, and in a courtyard the heroine is imploring the hero to stay with her (Fig. 84). Both the paintings illustrate the following poem of Keshav Dās:

> The spirits of the ancestors come, propitiate them,
> The past rushes to my brain! my love!
> Householders worship the *Durgās* nine,
> for success in life and salvation beyond.
> The kings accompanied by the *paṇḍits,*
> set out on tour to see their lands.

The skies are clear, the lotuses in bloom,
the nights are illuminated by the moon.
Lord Vishṇu and His consort Lakshmī,
are lost in their dance celestial.
In the month of *Āśvina*, the season of love,
why leave the home, why make me sad?

Kārttika

In the month of *Kārttika* the autumn moon shines with unusual brilliance and the souls of the lovers are filled with its radiance. Happy are the lovers who are together on the full moon night of October. Diwali, the Festival of Lamps, is celebrated. Millions of earthen lamps are lighted in all the towns and villages.

The lovers are seated on a terrace. In the background is a river in which people are bathing. The sky is clear and the rising sun is shown behind a hill (Fig. 86). The painting illustrates the month of *Kārttika* as described below by Keshav Dās:

Woods and gardens, rivers and lakes,
the earth itself and heavens above
All are clear and shining bright,
as if illumined by a million lamps
The days and nights are full of joy,
and couples are gambling
The walls and courtyards in every home
are gay with paintings of the gods.
The Universe is pervaded with celestial light,
all men and women are gay with love.
This is the month for earning merit
by alms-giving, worship of God and sacred baths
Therefore, I implore you, my love,
go not from home in *Kārttika*.

Agahana

The month of *Agahana* announces the arrival of winter. The days have shortened and the nights have lengthened. The sky is clear blue and there is a nip in the air. Beasts afraid of the approaching winter are seeking nooks and corners to hide themselves. Women are preparing for the winter, and buy new calico prints and card cotton for making quilts. The month of *Agahana* is shown in a delightful painting of the Kangra *Bārāmāsā* series in the form of lovers standing on a terrace by the lake side. A flight of cranes soaring upwards is shown in the sky (Plate XXIV). The painting illustrates the following poem of Keshav Dās:

Of all the months to God *Agahana* is most dear.
This is the month for happiness, and salvation of the soul.

The river banks are covered with flowers
And joyous notes of swans fill the air.
The days are neither cold nor hot,
How lucky to be together my love!
Do not therefore leave me alone
in *Agahana*, this lovely month of the year.

Pausha

"Enveloped by the mists of the month of *Pausha*, stained by dew, even on full moon nights the moon has no lustre. Its frozen disk is dim like a mirror tarnished by the breath. With its rays scarcely penetrating the fog, the sun, long after it has risen, continues to resemble the moon." Penetratingly cold is the surface of the lake and the river. "The wild elephant, though tormented by extreme thirst, withdraws its trunk suddenly, on coming in contact with the cold water. The water-fowl standing on the banks dare not enter the pond. Their cries can be heard, but they cannot be seen in the fog." Cold wind blows from the mountains and men and cattle seek warmth on the roofs of houses. *Kachnār* trees have shed their leaves, and their bare branches appear "like the naked swarthy *gopikās* of Vṛindāva-nam, whose clothes and jewels the Cloud-God has stolen in a divine mischief."

As the sun rises life quickens, and the villagers draped in blankets sit in sheltered sunny nooks of the courtyards of their houses and on roof-tops. The air is like champagne, bracing and invigorating. Draped in woollens the lovers are seated on a terrace. The snow-covered Dhauladhar is shown in the background. In the courtyard of a house, a man is receiving vigorous massage (Fig. 87). The painting illustrates the following poem of Keshav Dās:

Anything cold in the month of *Pausha*,
food, water, house, or dress,
Is liked by none anywhere.
Cold are the earth and the sky,
and the rich and poor all alike
Want sunshine, massage, betel, fire,
company of women, and warm clothes.
The days are short and nights are dark and long,
and this is the month for love.
Do not quarrel and turn away from me,
and leave me not this month of *Pausha*.

Māgha

The cold yields to slight warmth in the month of *Māgha*. The lady with hands folded implores her lover to stay at home. In the background is a grove with numerous birds perching on the branches. Music is being played in the courtyard of a house (Fig. 88). Keshav Dās thus describes the month of *Māgha:*

Forests and gardens echo the notes sweet
of peacock, pigeon, *koel* and *papīhā*

Endless is the humming of bees
The air is scented with musk, camphor, and sandal
Music is heard all through the night,
and all celebrate *Vasanta*
Do not leave the home in the month of *Māgha*
If you love me at all, my darling.

Phālguna

In the month of *Phālguna* there is warmth in the air, and lovers feel drowsy with amorous languor. Even days and nights have partaken of the colourfulness of *Phālguna*. *Phālguna* is the month of love, and the lovers long for *Phālguna* as the dark night longs for the full moon. The twisted *palāśa* trees, unworthy of notice in winter, shed their trifoliate leaves, and their twisted limbs get covered with dark-brown buds. As if touched by a magic wand, the buds open suddenly, and the trees are ablaze with flame-like orange-scarlet blossoms. Clad in the dazzling scarlet robe of *palāśa* flowers, the earth looks like a young bride.

In the Kangra Valley, the fields and hedges are dotted with snow-white blossoms of *kainth*, the wild pear. A small, unsightly, bushy tree a few days ago, in the last week of February, the wild pear flowers before the leaves unfurl, and becomes a dome of white blossoms. "I am the white song of creation", says the *kainth*. By the middle of March the young leaves open, fledging every tree with pale green silk, which provide garniture for clusters of silver white blossoms. In hedge-rows, the yellow blossoms of *Vasanta* are seen in profusion, and their pouting corollas are strangely significant of the Spring season. The pollen of flowers floats like a canopy toying with the southern breeze. Along the water-courses thousands of gentians with turquoise blue flowers provide a delightful frame to the fields of green wheat. In some of the fields blue flowers of linseed are mixed with yellow blossoms of *sarson*, providing a delightful colour contrast.

Swings are put up on the blossom-covered branches of trees in which bees are humming, enjoying the fragrance of the flowers. The Spring is in full bloom and great is love and joy. The water lily has found life and raised itself majestically. Jasmines open their buds and fill the air with their perfume. The sky is clear blue like the Mānasarovara lake, and the sun and the moon are its giant blossoms. Nature is quickened with a new birth and even inanimate things seem to feel a thrill. Pangs of love are born, and everything, everywhere looks for a mate.

The lover puts his left arm on the shoulders of the young lady, and looks at her fondly. The lady is clad in thin transparent muslin, and the palms of her hands are dyed red with henna. She is asking her lover to remain with her in the month of *Phālguna*. Near the terrace is a tree laden with flowers. In the background is a crowd of revellers playing Holī. A man with a drum leads the procession. Men are throwing *gulāl*, the red powder, on each other, while a woman standing on a terrace is sprinkling coloured water with a syringe over the men. It is thus that the month of *Phālguna* is represented in a *Bārāmāsā* Kangra painting (Fig. 89).

Keshav Dās describes the month of *Phālguna* as below:

All restraint gone
The rich and poor mix together
  and make merry.
Speech is free
  and there is no sense of shame.
Young men and women in every home
  play Holī, smearing each other with *gulāl*
  and fragrance of scented powders fills the air.
Why leave me alone, my love
  in *Phālguna*, the month for marry-making?

PLATES

PLATE I

THE LOTUS LADY

Padminī Nāyikā

Guler, *c.* 1800, size: 10×16·7 cm., Punjab Museum, Patiala

Classical romantic literature of the Hindus divides women into four types, and of these the *Padminī*, the Lotus, is the best of all. Malik Muhammad Jāyasī in his *Padmāvat* thus sums up the character of the *Padminī:* "The best kind of woman. She has the odour of lotus, thus attracting bees. She is not very tall or very short, very lean or very stout. She has four things long (hair, fingers, eyes and neck), four light (teeth, breasts, forehead and navel), and four thin (nose, loins, waist and thighs). Her face is like the moon. Her gait that of a swan. Her food is milk, and she is fond of betel and flowers. She has sixteen-sixteenths of all graces."

The lady, shown in the painting plucking plum blossoms, answers all qualifications required of a *Padminī Nāyikā*. In the full bloom of her youth and beauty, slender-waisted, with shapely breasts, well-proportioned shoulders, slender delicate hands and arms, moon-like face, dark expressive eyes, eyebrows like the bow of Kāma, and jet black hair, she is the Lady Lotus.

PLATE II

THE YOUNG BRIDE

Navoḍhā Nāyikā

Kangra, *c.* 1810, size: 12.5×16·7 cm., Bhārat Kalā Bhavan, Varanasi

Navoḍhā Nāyikā is the young bride. In this picture, a *navoḍhā* is shown being led into the bridal chamber, where her lord is anxiously awaiting her arrival. On her face is an expression of delight and hesitancy; she is on the threshold of married life and a strange experience awaits her. The young lady has bowed her head, and her face is partly veiled. The submissive grace of the *navoḍhā* seen in this picture is so typical of countless Indian brides, particularly in the rural area, which has as yet escaped modern education. Coomaraswamy's words might well describe this painting: "This picture is of most delicate and romantic loveliness and purity. There is a haunting charm in the gentle shyness of the bride as she is led by a friend to the bridal chamber. We may almost feel the wild beating of her heart and feel the tremulous touch of her red-stained fingers . . . The white marble building glistens in the moonlight. The whole picture bears the spell of that strange serenity and recollectedness, that so distinguish the old life of India."

Vidyāpati thus describes Rādhā as *Navoḍhā Nāyikā:*

With soft persuasion all the maidens
Led her to her lover's side,
A fawn ensnared from the forest
Panting hard.[25]

PLATE III

THE EXPERIENCED HEROINE

Prauḍhā Nāyikā

Kangra, *c.* 1825, size: 15·3 × 21·5 cm., Collection of Raja Dhruv Dev Chand of Lambagraon

This painting illustrates *Prauḍhā Nāyikā*, the mature and experienced heroine, the symbol of happy and harmonious married life.[26] The lovers are lying in close embrace, relaxed, satisfied and happy. The heroine's face with its expression of contented joy, her languor, and care-free abandonment to the impulse of love is symbolic of her maturity. She is the *prauḍhā*, the experienced *nāyikā*, mature in her experience of love.

The inscription on the painting reads:

प्रौढ़ा

लपटानी अति प्रेम सौं, दै उर उरज उतंग ।
घरी एक लों छुटेहुं पर, रही लगी सी अंग ।।

Lapṭānī ati prem saun, dai ura uraja utaṅga
Gharī ek lon chhuṭehuṅ par, rahī lagī sī aṅga

Passionately she embraces her lover
Pressing him to her heaving full bosom;
The grip loosens, but still
She appears to cling to him.

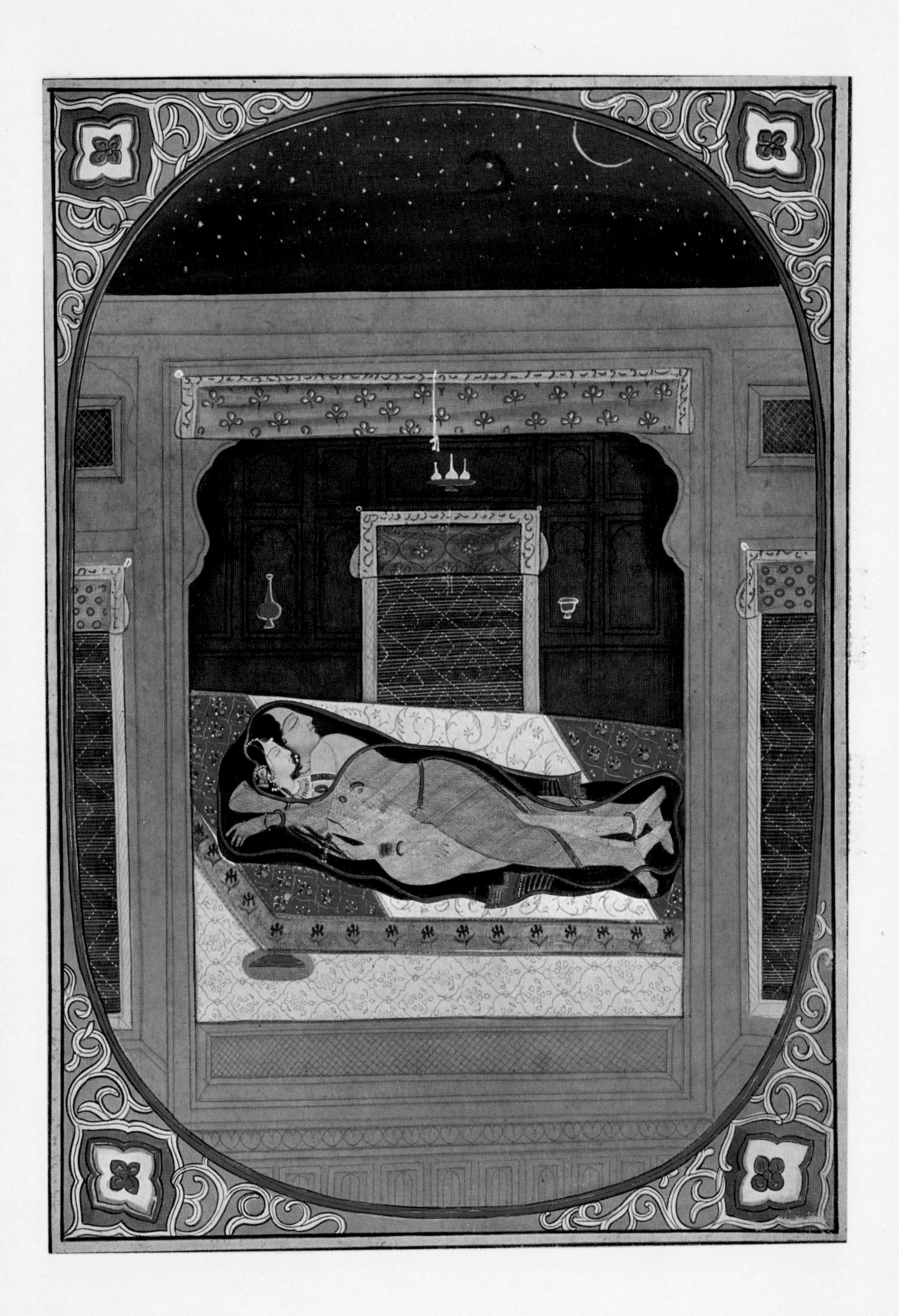

PLATE IV

THE DEVOTED HEROINE

Prauḍhā-dhīrā Nāyikā

Guler, *c.* 1790, size: 15 × 21 cm., National Museum, New Delhi

The painting from Guler illustrates the sweet, submissive, and affectionate Hindu wife, entirely dedicated to her husband. Her humility, grace and sweetness and mind enriched by suffering are eloquently shown in this painting. She is the *Prauḍhā-dhīrā Nāyikā*. The inscription on the back gives the following poem from the *Rasikapriyā* of Keshav Dās:

प्रौढ़ा सादरा धीरा

ग्रावत देखि लिये उठि ग्रागे ह्वै
केसव ग्रापनौ ग्रासन दीनौ ।
ग्रापही पानी पखारि भले जल
पानी कौ भाजन ल्याइ नवीनौ ।
बिरा बनाए के ग्रागे धरे जबि
ही कर कोमल बीजन लीनौ ।
बांह गही हरयें सै कह्यो हंसि
मैं तो इतौ ग्रपराध न कीनौ ।।

Āvata dekhi liye uṭhi āge hvai
Kesava āpanau āsan dinau,
Āpahī pānī pakhāri bhale jala
Pānī kau bhājan lyāi navīnau,
Birā banae ke āge dhare jabi
Hī kara komal bījana līnau,
Bānha gahī haryen sai kahyo hansi
Main to itau aparādha na kinau.

Seeing her lover come
She gets up and offers her seat to him.
She brings water and washes his feet;
Then offers betel, and picks up a fan to cool him.
Overwhelmed, he clutches her delicate hand
Saying, "Dear! does my offence need so much punishment?"

PLATE V

LOVERS BY THE LILY POOL

Rādhā's *Helā-hāva*

Guler, *c.* 1820, size: 17·5×22·8 cm., Municipal Museum, Allahabad

This is a delightful painting showing Rādhā's *Helā-hāva.* It is a moonlit night of autumn, and the lovers are meeting near a lotus pool. The reflection of the orb of the moon in the pool, and the trees covered by flowering creepers create an enchanting scene, which provides appropriate background to the romance of Rādhā and Kṛishṇa. Rādhā met Kṛishṇa in solitude in the moonlit night, with a smile on her face and fragrance around her. She then enslaved him by making him drink the wine of her lips. The method of continuous narration is followed, and the picture is in two parts: in the foreground is shown a love scene, and in the background the lovers are walking away with the hand of each on the other's shoulder. Kṛishṇa is with his favourite *gopī*, Rādhā. Rādhā with her beautiful moon-like face appears enchanting in the loveliness of her fresh youth. The dark Kṛishṇa and fair Rādhā, in close embrace, appear like the dark cloud, mated with a flash of lightning. The picture in the background is particularly enchanting; the lovers walking with the hand of one on the shoulder of the other symbolize companionship and deep intimacy. They are looking at each other fascinated and remind us of the lines of Vidyāpati:

> Her partridge-eyes beholding Kṛishṇa's moon-fair-face
> Were drinking draughts of dew:
> Each on the other gazing, spread abroad the taste of bliss.

WAITING FOR THE LOVER

Utkā Nāyikā

Guler, *c.* 1765, size: 17.8×24 cm., Kasturbhai Lalbhai Collection, Ahmedabad

The lady shown is the Expectant Heroine, *Utkā Nāyikā*, whose anxiety is roused greatly at her lover's inability to keep his appointment with her at the promised hour. She waits at the trysting place, and to relieve her anxiety occupies herself in decorating the trees with garlands of jasmine near the place of the expected meeting. In the stillness of the dark night, so admirably shown in this painting, one can almost hear the thumping of her excited heart. The deep blue sky is like a rich purple mass of collyrium. In the narrow horizon at the top is the star-spangled sky decorated by the pale orb of the moon.

PLATE VII

THE FORWARD

Abhisārikā Nāyikā

Kangra, *c.* 1830, size: 14·6×20·9 cm., Shrimati Sumati Morarjee Collection, Bombay

Abhisārikā is one who goes out to meet her lover. The one shown in this painting is a *Kṛishṇābhisārikā*, the *nāyikā* who goes out in a pitch dark night to meet her lover. The lover is shown on the left hand in a lighted room. The heroine is determinedly going forward ignoring rain and thunder. She has almost trodden on a cobra, who is hissing in anger. In the raging storm her blue *dupaṭṭā* is blown off her head. Her path is occasionally lighted by the flashes of lightning. Lightning is personified in Sanskrit poetry as the wife of the cloud, and has sympathy with the lady going for the assignation. The treatment of clouds and lightning is unique in this painting, almost modern in its simplicity.

PLATE VIII

THE LADY IN MOONLIGHT

Śuklābhisārikā Nāyikā

Guler, *c.* 1820, size: 17·2 × 21·1 cm., Jagmohandas K. Modi Collection, Bombay

The lady shown is *Śuklābhisārikā*, the one who goes out to meet her lover on a moonlit night. The moon has grown pale with shame at the lovelier brightness of the lady's face. The *chakoras* have forgotten the moon and are looking at the lovely face of the heroine, and are fascinated. Rādhā as *Śuklābhisārikā* is thus described by Guru Govind Singh in *Daśam Granth*, "Rādhikā went out in the moonlight in the light of the white soft moon, white everywhere, wearing a white robe to meet her Lord. She thus concealed herself in the white and roamed as the light itself in search of Him." The painting bears the following inscription:

छाकी प्रेम नेम में छबीली छैल
    छैल की बसुरिया के छलन छली गई ।
गहिरे गुलाबन के गहिरे गरूर गरे
    गोरी की गंध गैल गोकुल गली गई ।।
दर में दरीन हूं में दीपत दिवारी दरी
    दंत की दमक दुति दामिनि दली गई ।
चौसरि चवेली चारु चंचल चकोरन से
    चांदनी में चंद्रमुखी चौंकत चली गई ।।

Chhākī prema nema men chhabīlī chhaila
    Chhaila kī basuriyā ke chhalan chhalī gaī,
Gahire gulāban ke gahire garūr gare
    Gorī kī gandha gail Gokul galī gaī.
Dara men darīna hūn men dīpat divārī darī
    Dant kī damak duti dāmini dalī gaī,
Chausari chavelī chāru chañchal chakoran se
    Chāndanī men chandramukhī chaunkat chalī gaī.

The beautiful *nāyikā* rapt in love
Hears the call of the flute of her lover and goes out to meet him.
She is lovelier than the rose,
And her fragrance fills the streets of Gokul as she goes.
Her beauty shames the lighted lamps,
And the sparkle of her teeth dims the flash of lightning.
The moon-faced *nāyikā* with eyes more restless than the *chakora's*
Moves on through the moonlit night.

PLATE IX

RĀDHĀ'S COIFFURE

Kangra, *c.* 1790, size: 13.8×19·6 cm., Bhārat Kalā Bhavan, Varanasi

Rādhā is arranging her coiffure after a bath in the Yamunā. Smiling shyly, displaying her charms, she is busy with her toilet. This enchanting painting is out of a series illustrating the *Satsaiyyā* of Bihārī, possibly painted by Māṇak, the Kangra artist who painted the famous series of the *Gīta Govinda* paintings. The painting illustrates a poem of Bihārī given below:

कर समेटि कुच भुज उलटि, खएँ सीस-पटु टारि ।
काकौ मन बांधै न यह जूरा-बांधनहारि ।।

Kar sameṭi kuch bhuj ulaṭi, khain sīs-paṭu ṭāri,
Kākau man bāndhai na yeh jūṛā-bāndhan-hāri.

Her arms thrown back, the end of her *sārī* on her shoulder,
The lovely damsel tying her hair, whose heart will she not twist into knots!

PLATE X

TOILET OF RĀDHĀ

Guler, *c.* 1785, size: 13·4×19.3 cm.. Collection of Gopi Krishna Kanoria, Calcutta

This painting shows the toilet of Rādhā. In the background are three blossoming shrubs, symbol of the blooming youth of the lady. Two maid-servants are holding a white sheet of cloth to screen her, and another is wiping her wet feet with a towel. At the back is another, holding bottles of scented oil. In front are scattered ewers with long spouts, which Archer would interpret as symbols of her ardent desire and love-longings. The lady's face is charming, her dark, expressive eyes, pencilled eyebrows, delicate nose, and a wealth of long glossy black hair, providing a frame for her lovely breasts which remind one of the following poem of Vidyāpati:

"A joyous day this day for me!
I saw my love when she was bathing,
A stream of water pouring from her hair,—
The clouds were showering strings of pearls!

Wiping her face intentifly,
As though she cleansed a golden mirror,—

Discovering both her breasts,
Where had been set inverted golden cups,

She let her zone fall free:
That was the bound of my desire, says Vidyāpati."[27]

PLATE XI

THE MEETING OF EYES

Guler, *c.* 1810, size: 15 × 20.3 cm., Collection of Raja Dhruv Dev Chand of Lambagraon

The lover is looking from a window in a marble pavilion, when the lady surrounded by her female companions is crossing the courtyard. While with one hand she is holding the *dupaṭṭā* which has slipped from her head, with the other she is playing with the *chakrī*. As she looks up, their eyes meet, and desire for union is awakened. Birds are symbolically introduced to create the atmosphere of love; a pair of ducks are in the foreground, and on the wall behind the lady are two pigeons making love. The inscription on the painting is given below:

मंद मुसुकाति है सकाति गुरु लोकनि पै
   चितै त्रसी सी वन हरिनी ज्यों जाल कों ।
भोंह की मचनि युग नैनन की नचनि नाथ
   कुच की उचनि पै हलनि मोती माल कों ।।
अंचल चलन त्यों ही भुज की लचन चारु
   कंठ की मुरन उछरन करताल कों ।
सखिन कौं टेरति मनोज मन घेरति है,
   चकरीन फेरति ए हेरति है लाल कों ।।१।।

Manda musukāti hai sakāti guru lokani pai
   Chitai trasī sī vana harinī jyon jāla kaun,
Bhonh kī machani yuga nainana kī nachani Nāth
   Kuch kī uchani pai halani motī māla kaun.
Añchal chalan tyon hī bhuja kī lachan chāru
   Kaṇṭha kī muran uchharan karatāl kaun,
Sakhin kaun ṭerati manoja mana gherati hai,
   Chakrīn ferati ae herati hai lāla kaun.

A smile plays on her lips.
The eyes dance, the brows move, the neck swings,
The breasts heave supporting the pearl necklace.
One hand keeps the yo-yo in play;
   the other is busy lifting the slipping fold of the *sārī*.
She calls out to her companions thus trying to
   attract the attention of her lover.
And she plays with the yo-yo,
   while stealing glances at her lover.

PLATE XII

MĀNINI NĀYIKĀ

Kangra, *c.* 1800, size: 15.7 × 20 cm., National Museum, New Delhi

Another phase of 'Love in Separation' is determined by *Māna*, which implies coldness, stubbornness, pride or caprice. *Māna* may be slight, moderate, or heavy. While slight *māna* may be overcome by coaxing and cajoling by the companion of the lady, the heavy *māna* is only overcome when the lover humbles himself, and falls at the feet of the lady. This is a phase which comes in the love life of most lovers. Plates XII and XIII represent *Māninī Nāyikās*.

In this painting the lover is shown in the pavilion sitting in front of a fountain surrounded by two lamps. The companions of the lady are coaxing and cajoling her to relent, and one in extreme humility is even touching her feet. The inscription on the painting is as below:

समझ सिआनी तें अयानी होत घरी घरी
  नाहीं नाहीं कहत नेंक न अघात है ।
कै है घरवास कह्यो मान स्यामा स्यामै मिल
  बिछुरे तें अमर बेल सोऊ मुरझात है ।
जानत न हार जीत मानत न परतीत
  कौन रसरीत वारों बोलत रिसात है ।
उनको तो विरही की विधा विथुरात बलि
  तू तो इतरात इत रात बीत जात है ।

Samajha siyānī ten ayānī hota gharī gharī
 Nāhīn nāhīn kahata nenka na aghāta hai,
Kai hai gharavāsa kahyo mān syāmā syāmai mila
 Bichhure ten *amar bela* soū murajhāta hai.
Jānata na hāra jīta mānata na paratīta
 Kaun rasarīta vāron bolat risāt hai,
Unako to virahī kī vidhā vithurāta bali
 Tū to itarāta ita rāta bīta jāta hai.

Oh wise *sakhī*, why be so indifferent; why be adamant?
You know not where victory lies, nor heed my advice.
How should I speak to you, when every word, I say, irritates you?
He is pining in separation, and you are drunk with pride!
Even the *amar bela* dries up in separation.
Go to Śyāma; the night is passing swiftly.

PLATE XIII

THE OBDURATE LADY

Māninī Nāyikā

Kangra, *c.* 1800, size: 15.2 × 22.3 cm., National Museum, New Delhi

This is an instance of extreme obduracy, known as *Guru Māna*. It is a delightful night with dark clouds in the sky lighted by flashes of lightning. The lover who is shown in the form of Kṛishṇa in the chamber below has sent a garland and flowers to the lady. The *Māninī* refuses not only the direct prayers of the lover, but also the messages of love sent through a messenger. She has thrown the garland and the flowers on the ground, and is seated with bent back, hanging head and averted face. A girl companion is pointing towards the dark cloud, while the one in front is coaxing and cajoling her. The girl messenger below is reporting the failure of all efforts to persuade the lady to meet him. The painting illustrates the following poem by Keshav Dās, which is inscribed on the back:

कबित्त

सिखै हारी सखी डरपाय हारी कादंबनी
  दामिनि दिखाय हारी दिसि अधरात की।
झुकि झुकि हारी रति मारि मारि हार्यो मार
  हारी झकझोरति त्रिविध गति बात की ।।
दई निरदई दई बाहि ऐसी काहे मति
  जारति जु रैन दिन दाह ऐसे गात की।
कैसे हू न मानै हों बुलाई हारी केशोराय
  बोलि हारी कोकिला बुलाई हारी चातकी ।।

Sikhai hārī sakhī ḍarpāi hārī kādambanī
  Dāmini dikhāi hārī disi adharāt kī,
Jhuki jhuki hārī Rati māri māri hāryo Mār
  Hārī jhakajhorati trividha gati bāt kī.
Daī niradaī daī bāhi aisī kāhe mati
  Jārati ju rain dina dāha aise gāta kī,
Kaise hū na mānai haun bulāī hārī Keśorāi
  Boli hārī kokilā bulaī hārī chātakī.

All the persuasion of the *sakhīs* has failed
  to reconcile her to her lover.
The dark clouds too could not frighten her,
And lightning flashed in vain to show the
  way in the gloom of the night.
The fragrant breeze, the cooing of the *koel* and the *chātakī*,
And even the efforts of Kāma, the God of Love,
  and his consort, Rati, have failed.
She burns day and night in the fire of separation,
But cruel Providence would not have pity on her.

PLATE XIV

AUGURY OF THE CROW

Kangra, *c.* 1800, size: 14.8 × 21.5 cm., Collection of Raja Dhruv Dev Chand of Lambagraon

The *nāyikā* shown in this painting is *Vāsakasajjā*, one, who desirous of union with her lord, stands at the doorstep waiting for him. She is asking the crow perching on the pomegranate bush to fly away.[28] Her daughters are on the terrace looking for their returning father. The love-lit eyes, heaving breasts peeping out of the *pesvāj*, and extended arms convey her feelings of joyous expectancy. The straight and pointed cypress, and the minarets represent her ardent desire. This lovely painting from the collection of the Raja of Lambagraon was apparently executed by one of the master artists of Maharaja Sansar Chand at Alampur. In the distance across the river is shown the palace at Tira perched on a mountain top.

PLATE XV

LADY ON A SWING

Kangra, *c.* 1790, size: 14.3 × 21.5 cm., National Museum, New Delhi

In the stuffy heat of the rainy season following spells of rain, it is a delight to sway in a swing. In the 18th century France swings were invented, for the skirts were too long, and the swings swept up the skirts in the breeze to the delight of the beaux below. In the paintings of Fragonard such scenes are commonly shown. In India, however, a swing was a genuine necessity for cooling the body, particularly in an age when electric fans were not known. In this painting, the lady, attended by her servants and companions, is enjoying the swing.

PLATE XVI

ADMIRING THE RAIN CLOUDS

Guler, *c.* 1810, size: 14·1 × 17·5 cm., Kasturbhai Lalbhai Collection, Ahmedabad

The rainy season has a special appeal for lovers in India. The white cranes, silhouetted against the background of dark clouds, are an unforgettable sight. The music of flowing water and the patter of rain-drops have a strange fascination. In this painting, the lady is pointing towards the skein of *sāras* cranes cleaving the dark clouds with their golden legs. The beautiful sight of the cranes, and the cool breeze, which heralds rain, have raised ardent desire in her. She is restless and is desirous of entering the adjoining bed-chamber, and at the same time she also lingers a while not to miss the beauty of the sight of the white cranes providing such a heavenly contrast to the *kṛishṇa*-blue clouds. This is a good illustration of *saṁyoga*, love in union.

The *dohā* on the painting is as below:

संयोग

छिनक चलत ठठकत छिनक, भुज प्रीतम गल डार।
चढ़त अटा देखति घटा, बिज्जु छटा सी नार।।

Chhinaka chalat ṭhaṭhakat chhinaka, bhuja prītam gala ḍāra,
Chaḍhata aṭā dekhati ghaṭā, bijju chhaṭā sī nāra.

With her arm around her lover's neck,
She watches the dark gathering clouds from the top of the house,
Restless and shining like a streak of lightning,
Sometimes she moves on, and then stops suddenly.

PLATE XVII

SHELTERING FROM RAIN

Kangra, *c.* 1800, size: 14.6 × 20.4 cm., Punjab Museum, Patiala

One of the most delightful paintings by the master-artist of the paintings of the *Bhāgavata Purāṇa* series, it shows 'Love in Union'. Kṛishṇa was grazing cows along with the cowherd boys and *gopīs* when it started raining suddenly. They all took shelter under a pair of trees. While a cowherd boy protected himself from rain with a lotus-leaf, another one hid among the trunks. Kṛishṇa and his favourite *gopī* sheltered beneath a common black shawl. The cows are providing a cover to the lovers. A liana is embracing the *tamāla* tree in its coils, and the trees themselves are locked in embrace. On the crown of a tree, a peacock, the lover of the cloud, is shouting exultantly. In a corner is a skein of snow-white *sāras* cranes soaring into the sky. On the left are two *gopīs* carrying pitchers. What the one to the extreme left is saying to the other is expressed in the following poem of the poet Bahādur:

मल्लिका चारु चुभी चित चंपक, नागलता मिली ताल तमालन ।
सागर सों सरिता सिगरी ललना, बस प्रेम के ह्वै निज लालन ।।
काजर से घन में चपला चहुं ओर नची रचि चंचल चालन ।
बाल तुम्हें बलि जैहों बहादर, आजि मिलौ चलि काहे गुपालन ।।

Mallikā chāru chubhī chita chaṁpaka,
  nāgalatā milī tāla tamālana.
Sāgara saun saritā sigarī lalanā,
  basa prem ke hvai nija lālana.
Kājara se ghana men chapalā
  chahun ora nachī rachi chañchal chālana,
Bāla tumhen bali jaihon Bahādur,
  āji milau chali kāhe Gupālana.

The jasmine is entwined with the *champaka*,
The *nāgalatā* is embracing the *tamāla*;
The rivers are rushing madly to mate with the ocean,
And young women overcome with
  passion are seeking their lovers.
The restless lightning is dancing in the dark clouds.
May you also be blessed with love, Oh *sakhī!*

PLATE XVIII

TRYST IN THE FOREST

Kangra, *c.* 1800, size : 14.2×20.3 cm., Collection of Miss Alice Boner, Varanasi

Rādhā and Kṛishṇa met at the tryst on the outskirts of the village. As they stood on the bed of leaves, there was a flash of lightning in the dark cloud, and it started drizzling. Kṛishṇa raised his dark blanket to protect Rādhā from rain. This is a painting of rare beauty expressive of the tenderness of love.

PLATE XIX

LOVE IN MOONLIGHT

Guler, *c.* 1820, size: 16.5 × 21.3 cm., Bhārat Kalā Bhavan, Varanasi

The autumn moon shines with unusual brilliance and the souls of the lovers are filled with its radiance. Happy are the lovers who are together on the full moon night of *Kārttika*. The lovers are intoxicated with joy, their red-streaked eyes, brimming with passion. The *sakhīs* watch their sports from a corner of the garden. Immersed deep in the ocean of *rasa*, they gaze at each other ardently, and sit with arms round each other's neck in the pavilion in the garden, colouring it a glossy brown with the lustre of their figures, which, melting in ecstasies, can hardly bear the weight of their necklaces, rings and the sandal-paint. The eyes of Rādhā, dripping with love, become cool when they gaze at the Lord, and then they begin to look like a pair of golden lotus-buds sparkling with pale lustre beneath the surface of the water. At the sight of Kṛishṇa, and the moon of Vraja, they unfold their petals in unspeakable glory.

This is a painting in which love in union is shown against a background of architectural splendour. The marble pavilion, the lovers' nest, is studded with precious stones. The sky is beautifully jewelled by the moon and below it are the *sakhīs* talking about the course of love of Rādhā and Kṛishṇa. Rādhā is a dream of feminine beauty, her dark, expressive eyes, coy expression, and projecting breasts bursting out of the *cholī*, with their beauty enhanced by the necklace of pearls and diamonds. This is a painting of timeless beauty eloquently depicting the joy of love in union.[29]

The painting bears an inscription in Gurmukhi on the top. Possibly, it was painted by a Guler artist for a Sikh patron. The poem is as below:

Swayīa:

Bhookhan bheda swār sabhey aṅga
Auré bhānt kiyo kūchh bānā
Chandan kī kañchukī kuch ūpar
Kesarband teū raṅg ṭhānā.
Śrī Ghanaśyāma sujān piyā
Raske chaske kūchh bheda na jānā
Ho tirchhī dehsī lalnā tab
Kañchukī kholat lāl lajānā.

Rādhā decorated herself with a variety of ornaments,
Dressed in a unique manner,
And covered her breasts with a saffron-colour bodice,
fragrant with sandal.
Śrī Kṛishṇa in joyous abandon was immersed
in the ocean of pleasure.
The beloved averted her face, bent aside,
And Kṛishṇa boldly unlaced her bodice.

PLATE XX

LOVE IN A GARDEN PAVILION

Kangra, *c.* 1810, size: 20 × 25.4 cm., Collection of Raja Dhruv Dev Chand of Lambagraon

This is a rare example of an illustration of a poem of Sūr Dās by a Kangra artist. How the artist loved the poem is evident from the inscription on the back of the painting where letters are inscribed on white clouds surrounded by a haze of gold. The sun has risen in the east, and Rādhā and Kṛishṇa come out of the pavilion in the garden after spending the night together. Rādhā clad in a blue *sārī* is holding Kṛishṇa's hand — an expression of deep intimacy. Hers is a face of exquisite sensibility, with a beautiful chin, delicate lips, shapely nose, and languorous eyes. The lovers are looking at each other enraptured.

The marble pavilion, studded with precious stones, is surrounded by a grove of trees on which pairs of love-birds are warbling music. In the foreground is a lotus lake with half-opened lotus flowers and buds. In a corner, a *chakvā* is flying to his mate after the night-long separation. This exquisite painting from the collection of the Raja of Lambagraon was painted by one of Maharaja Sansar Chand's most accomplished artists. The inscription is reproduced below:

कुंज भवन तें निकसे भोरहिं स्यामा स्याम खरे। जलद नवीन तरुन दामिनि मिलि बरस निसा उघरे।।
गौर स्याम तन नील पीत पट आरस चितहि धरे। श्रमजल बूंद कहूं कहूं उडगन बादर में निकरे।।
प्रेमप्रवाह छुटी जनु सरिता टूटी माल गरे। काजर अधरत बोल नैनन रंग अंग झील भरे।।
भूषन विविध हुते मतवारे आरस उमगि ढरे। सोभा अतिहि विलोक सूर प्रभु नांही जात टरे।।

Kuñja bhavan ten nikase bhorahin syāmā syāma khare,
Jalada navīn taruna dāmini mili baras nisā ughare.
Gaur syāma tana nīla pīta paṭa āras chitahi dhare,
Śramajal būnda kahūn kahūn uḍagana bādara men nikare.
Prempravāh chhuṭī janu saritā ṭūṭī māla gare,
Kājara adharata bola nainan raṅga aṅga jhīla bhare.
Bhūshana vividha hute matavāre āras umagi ḍhare,
Sobhā atihi viloka Sūra Prabhu nāhin jāta ṭare.

The day has dawned, and Kṛishṇa and Rādhā come out
of the garden pavilion in which the night was spent.
Rādhā is wearing a blue *sārī*; Kṛishṇa is in his yellow ***pītāmbara.***
They are relaxed and suffused with the fulfilment of love.
Their garlands are broken;
Beads of sweat shine on Kṛishṇa's limbs like stars
peeping through the clouds;
The collyrium in Rādhā's eyes has trickled to the lips,
And the vermilion on her lips has spread to the eyes;
The ornaments on her person are displaced in their
joyous abandon,
It looks as though a mighty cloud
And impetuous lightning have come to rest after
their night-long play.

PLATE XXI

THE MONTH OF CHAITRA

Kangra, *c.* 1790, size: 14.5 × 20.3 cm., Collection of Raja Dhruv Dev Chand of Lambagraon

Plates XXI, XXII, and XXIV are from the famous *Bārāmāsā* series of paintings, originally in the collection of Maharaja Sansar Chand. In this painting, the lovers are seated on a terrace, and in the background are flowering shrubs and trees in which birds of many kinds are warbling music. The lady is describing the charm of *Chaitra* (March-April), and exhorting her husband to remain at home.

The painting illustrates the following poem of Keshav Dās from the *Kavipriyā:*

अथ चैत वर्णनं

छप्पय–
फूली लतिका ललित तरुनि तर फूले तरुवर।
फूली सरिता सरस सुभग फूले सब सरवर।।
फूली कामनि, कामरूपकरि कंतनि पूजहिं।
सुक सारो कुल कलित, फूलि कोकिल कल कूजहिं।।
कहि केसव ऐसे फूल महि फूलहि सूलन लाइए।
पिय आपु चलन की का चली सु चित्तन चैत चलाइए।।१।।

Phūlī latikā lalita taruni tara phūle taruvara,
Phūlī saritā saras subhaga phūle sab saravara.
Phūlī kāmani, kāmarūpakari kantani pūjahin,
Suka sāro kula kalita, phūli kokila kala kūjahin.
Kahi Kesava aise phūla mahi phūlahi sūlana lāie,
Piya āpu chalan kī kā chalī su chittana Chaita chalāie.

Lovely creepers are in bloom, blossoming
  trees are young once more,
And streams and lakes are full of flowers.
Women, aglow with passion, dressed in their best,
Abandon themselves to sports of love.
The parrot, the *mainā* and the *koel* are singing songs of love.
Why think of going away, why spoil this joy
  in the month of Chaitra, my love?

PLATE XXII

THE MONTH OF ŚRĀVAṆA

Kangra, *c.* 1790, size: 14.5 × 20.3 cm., Collection of Raja Dhruv Dev Chand of Lambagraon

This is a delightful illustration of the rainy month of *Śrāvaṇa*. The lovers are seated on a *chaukī* and the lady is pointing towards the flash of lightning in the cloud. On a rounded hillock a peacock is shouting with joy, hailing the clouds, and in the background is a flight of white *sāras* cranes soaring into the sky. A mountain stream is winding sinuously through the hillocks. In a corner is Alampur with the garden palace of Sansar Chand.

The inscription on the painting from the *Kavipriyā* of Keshav Dās is as below:

अथ सावन वर्णनं

छप्पय–
केसव सरिता सकल मिलत सागर मन मोहें ।
ललित लता लपटात तरुन तन तरवर सोहें ।।
चित चपला मिलि मेघ चपल चमकत चहुं ओरन ।
मन भावन कहं भेंटि भूमि कूजत मिस मोरन ।।
इहि रीति रमन रमनीन कहुं रमन उर लगै रमावन ।
पिय गमन करन की को कहै गमन सुनिय नहिं सावन ।।५।।

Kesava saritā sakal milat sāgar man mohain
Lalita latā lapaṭāt taruna tana taravar sohain.
Chita chaplā mili megha chapala chamakat chahun oran,
Man bhāvana kahan bhenṭi bhūmi kūjata misa moran.
Ihi rīti raman ramanīn kahun raman ura lagai ramāvan,
Piya gaman karan kī ko kahai gaman suniya nahin Sāvan.

The streams look so lovely as they rush to meet the sea.
The creepers enchant the eye embracing young trees lovingly.
The lightning flashes restlessly as she sports with rolling clouds.
The peacocks with their shrill cries announce
the mating of earth and sky.
All lovers meet in this month of Sāvan,
why forsake me then, my love?

PLATE XXIII

THE MONTH OF BHĀDON

Guler, *c.* 1810, size: 15 × 22·3 cm., State Museum, Lucknow

Different series of *Bārāmāsā* paintings exist, and this picture, from another series by a Guler artist, illustrates the rainy month of Bhādon (August-September). The lovers are seated in a balcony of a house in a garden watching a flight of cranes. On hearing the thunder-clap following a flash of lightning the lady embraces her lover.

Keshav Dās thus describes the month of Bhādon:

अथ भाद्र वर्णनं

छप्पय–
घोरत घन चहुं ओर घोष निर्घोषनि मंडहिं ।
धाराधर धरि धरनि मुसल धारनि जल छंडहिं ।।
झिल्लीगन झंकार पवन झुकि झुकि झकझोरत ।
सिंह बाघ गुंजरत पुंज कुंजर तरु तोरत ।।
निसि दिन विसेष निःसेष मति जात, सु ओलो ओडिए ।
देस पियूषर विदेस विष भादों भवन न छोड़िए ।।६।।

Ghorat ghan chahun ora ghosh nirghoshani maṇḍahin,
Dhārādhar dhari dharani musal dhārani jal chhaṇḍahin.
Jhillīgan jhaṅkār pavan jhuki jhuki jhakajhorat,
Sinh bāgh guñjarat puñj kuñjar taru torat.
Nisi din visesh niḥsesh mati jāt, su olo oḍie,
Des piyūshar vides vish Bhādon bhavan na chhoḍiye.

The purple clouds are gathering, the thunder
rolls and rain pours in torrents.
The wind blows fiercely, the cicadas chirp,
the lions roar, and elephants fell the trees.
The day is dark like the night, and
one's own home is the best.
Pray leave me not in the month of Bhādon
for separation pains like poison.

PLATE XXIV

THE MONTH OF MĀRGASĪRSHA (AGAHANA)

Kangra, *c.* 1790, size: 14·5 × 20·3 cm., Collection of Raja Dhruv Dev Chand of Lambagraon

The painting illustrates the early winter month of Agahana (November-December), when the sky is clear and swans migrate from the mountains to the plains. The lovers are standing on a terrace overlooking a lake in which water-birds are disporting. A hamlet nestles on the top of a hill reminding one of the Kangra Valley and its charming villages. In the sky is a flight of swans soaring into the sky. The painting illustrates the following poem of Keshav Dās:

अथ मार्गशीर्ष वर्णनं

छप्पय–
मासन में हरि अंस कहत यासों सब कोई।
स्वारथ परमारथनि देत भारथ में दोई।।
केसव सरिता सकल कूल फूले सुगंध गुर।
कूजित कल कलहंस, कलित कलहंसनि के सुर।।
दिन परम नरम सीत न गरम, करम करम यह पाइ ऋतु।
करि प्राननाथ परदेस कहं मारगसिर मारग न चितु।।६।।

Māsan men Hari aṁsa kahat yāson sab koī,
Svāratha paramārathani det bhārath men doī.
Kesava saritā sakal kool phoole sugandh gur,
kūjit kal kalahaṁs kalit kalahamsani ke sur.
Din param naram sīt na garam, karam karam yah pāi ṛitu,
Kari prānnāth pardes kahan Māragsir mārag na chitu.

Of all the months to God Agahana is most dear.
This is the month for happiness and salvation of the soul.
The river banks are covered with flowers
And joyous notes of swans fill the air.
The days are neither cold nor hot,
How lucky to be together my love!
Do not, therefore, leave me alone in Agahana,
this lovely month of the year.

PLATE XXV

THE MONTH OF PAUSHA

Guler, *c.* 1830, size: 15.3 × 22 cm., Kasturbhai Lalbhai Collection, Ahmedabad

This painting is from a series illustrating the *Bārāmāsā* of Keshav Dās, describing the twelve months. The month illustrated is Pausha (December), when it is intensely cold in the hills of the Punjab. The lovers are snuggling in a common blanket, with a brazier in front of them. Sitting in companionship, and looking into each other's eyes, the lovers are enraptured, and remind us of a song from *Annam*.

It is late at night
As we talk gently,
Sitting by one another,
Life is as beautiful as night.[30]

The inscription on the painting is in Gurmukhi script. The cypresses alternating with mangoes is a convention of Guler artists. It seems that this painting is from a series prepared for a Sikh patron by a Guler artist. The inscription is as below:

पूस वर्णन

छप्पय–
शीतल, जल, थल, बसन, असन शीतल अनरोचक।
केशवदास अकास अवनि शीतल असुमोचक।।
तेल, तूल, तामोर, तपन, तापन, नव नारी।
राज रंक सब छोड़ि करत इनहीं अधिकारी।।
लघु दिवस दीह रजनी रमन होत दुसह दुख रूस में।
यह मन क्रम बचन विचारि पिय पंथ न बूझिय पूस में।।

Śītal jala, thala, basan, asan śītal anarochaka,
Keshavadās akās avani śītal aśumochaka.
Tel, tūla, tāmor, tapan, tāpan, nava nārī,
Rāja raṅka sab chhoḍi, karat inhin adhikārī.
Laghu divasa dīha rajanī raman hota dusah dukh rūs men,
Yah mana, krama, bachana vichāri piya
pantha na būjhiya Pus men.

This is the month of Pausha when none likes
cold food, light clothes and chilly places.
The skies and the earth breathe cold.
In this month everyone, whether rich or poor,
wants to have six things: oil massage, warm
clothes, betel, sunshine, company of young
women and a warm hearth.
The days are short and the nights long,
And this is the season for love. Do not turn
away; that would be most painful.
Stay (at home) and be with me.[31]

BIRDS, INSECTS, TREES, SHRUBS AND CLIMBERS MENTIONED IN SANSKRIT AND HINDI LITERATURE

BIRDS

CHAKORA: *Alectoris graeca*, a Himalayan partridge, the lover of the moon, said to feed on the rays of the moon.

CHAKRAVĀKA: *Casarca ferruginea*, a variety of duck, also called *chakavā (surkhāb)*. Legend relates that pairs of these birds are souls of two sinning lovers who are said to sleep apart at night, and call endlessly to one another, "Chakavā, may I come?", "No, Chakavī".

CHĀTAKA: *Cuculus melanoleucas*, a type of swallow said to drink only rain drops as they fall from clouds.

CROW: *Corvus splendens*, messenger of separated lovers; also a scavenger who eats leavings and filth.

GARUḌA: A mythical bird with parrot's head, human body and clawed feet, the vehicle of Vishṇu, and enemy of serpents.

HAṀSA: *Phoenicopterus ruber*, the flamingo, and also the goose, *Anser indicus*.

KHAÑJANA: *Motacilla maderaspatensis*, the wag-tail, symbol of restlessness, and also of eyes of the beloved.

KOEL: *Eudynamis scolopaceus*, a dark bird commonly found in mango gardens during the flowering and fruiting periods. Its cry is *kuhu, kuhu, kuhu*, rising in scale with each successive call, and its *pañchama*-note is the dominant of Nature's chorus.

KOONJA: *Anthropoides virgo*, the demoiselle crane.

KRAUÑCHA: *Numenius arquata*, curlew.

MAINĀ: *Acridotheres tristis*, a cage bird, is a good mimic.

NĪLAKAṆṬHA: *Coracias benghalensis*, roller or blue jay, sacred to Vishṇu.

PAPĪHĀ: *Hierococcyx varius*, commonly known as the hawk-cuckoo, or the brain-fever bird — its cry is '*Pī kahān*', — 'Where is my love?'

PARROT: *Psittacula eupatria*, a pet bird said to overhear conversation of lovers, and to repeat it in awkward circumstances.

PEACOCK: *Pavo cristatus*, male is said to be lover of the clouds, delights in rain.

SĀRAS: *Antigone antigone*, the slate-coloured sāras crane, said to pair for life, and hence a symbol of devoted love.

INSECTS AND MITES

ANT: *Camponotus compressus*, the common black ant, symbol of industry and patience, called *Pipīlikā* in Sanskrit.

BHRAMARA: Bumble bees, *Xylocopa aestuans* in the plains, and *Bombus orientalis* in the hills. Lovers of flowers, symbol of the male.

BIRBAHUTI: *Trombidium gigas*, *Indragopaka* (Sanskrit), the velvet mite of scarlet-colour. They appear in large numbers in early rains.

JAGNU: *Lamprophorus tenebrosus*, and *Luciola gorhami*, light producing insects belonging to the family Lampyridae.

LĀKSHĀ: *Laccifer lacca*, the lac insect.

MADHU MAKSHIKĀ: Honey-bees, of which *Apis indica* is docile, and *Apis dorsata* is ferocious, nesting in the open on high trees and arches.

PATAṄGA: Applicable to many species of flying insects attracted to light.

TREES, SHRUBS AND CLIMBERS

AGURU : *Aquilaria agallocha*, a large evergreen tree with fragrant heart-wood.

AMALTĀS : *Cassia fistula*, a small hardy tree with pendulous racemes of large bright yellow flowers in April and May.

ARJUNA : *Terminalia arjuna*, a large shady tree.

AŚOKA : *Saraca indica*, a herald of spring, has scarlet crimson bunches of flowers in early March. Said to flower on the touch of a beautiful woman's feet.

ATIMUKTA : *Jasminum sp.*

BANDHŪKA : *Pentapetes phoenicia* (or *Leucas linifolia*)

BETEL : *Piper betle*, *pān*, *tāmbūla*, a climber, leaves used for chewing.

BIMBA : *Momordica coccinia*, a climber with bright red fruit.

CHAMPAKA : *Michelia champaka*, a large tree commonly grown in temples, with light yellow fragrant flowers.

DEVADĀRU : *Cedrus deodara*, the Himalayan cedar.

GANDHARĀJA : *Gardenia florida*, a shrub with highly fragrant white flowers.

GUÑJA : *Abrus precatorius*, seeds used as jeweller's weights.

GUL MOHUR : *Delonix regia*, an umbrella-like tree with pinnate feathery leaves. It bears scarlet flowers in May.

HONEY-APPLE : *Aegle marmelos*, *bel*, *śrīphala*, 'Bengal quince', a large round fruit.

JASMINE : Several varieties are mentioned, as *chamelī*, Arabian jasmine, *Jasminum sambac*; *champaka*, *Michelia champaka*; *mālatī*, clover-scented jasmine, *Aganosma caryophyllata* (or perhaps *F. grandiflorum*); *kunda* Indian jasmine, *Jasminum pubescens.*

JUJUBE : *Zizyphus jujuba*, *beri*, small round fruits, favourites of boys.

KACHNĀR : *Bauhinia variegata*, a medium sized ornamental tree with drooping branches. It produces a rich harvest of mauve or white blossoms in February-March.

KADAMBA : *Anthocephalus indicus*—ball-like flowers in rains, favourite of Kṛishṇa.

KANDALĪ : *Aneilema nudiflorum*, an annual herb with blue purple flowers in the rainy season.

KARṆIKĀRA : *Pterospermum acerifolium*, a large tree with broad leaves.

KĀŚA : *Saccharum spontaneum*, a tall grass.

KESARA : *Crocus sativa*, safflower, a herald of spring.

KETAKĪ : *Pandanus odoratissimus*, screw-pine — a highly fragrant plant with spinous sword-like pointed leaves.

KIṀŚUKA : *Butea frondosa*, *Palāśa*, *Dhak* — tree with beautiful crimson-red flowers, a herald of spring.

KOVIDĀRA : *Bauhinia purpurea*, a small tree bearing pink flowers in November.

KUMUDA : *Nymphaea esculenta*, a water lily with white flowers opening at night time, and closing during the day.

KUNDA : *Jasminum pubescens*, a jasmine.

KURABAKA : *Lawsonia alba*, also called *mehendee*, crushed leaves used for dyeing palms of hands.

KUṬAJA : *Wrightia zeylanica*, a small tree with white flowers.

LAVAṄGA-VINE : *Limonia scandens*, *lavaṅga-latā* — a herald of spring.

LODHRA : *Symplocos racemosa*, pollen used as face powder in ancient India.

LOTUS and WATER-LILY : Many varieties are mentioned, as *aravinda* and *kamala* which are day-flowering, and *kubalaya* and *kumudinī*, which flower at night. *Nelumbium speciosum* is the common lotus. *Utpala* (Sk.) is the blue water lily, *Nymphaea coerulea.*

MĀDHAVĪ : *Hiptage madhablota*, a scandent shrubby climber, herald of spring, and lover of the mango tree.

MAHUĀ : *Bassia latifolia*, a common shade tree in Central India. An alcoholic beverage is distilled from its flowers.

MĀLATĪ : *Jasminum grandiflorum*, a twining shrub with fragrant white flowers.

MANDĀRA : *Erythrina indica*, small tree with red flowers in leafless condition in early March.

MANGO : *Mangifera indica*, tender shoots and herald of spring, flowers in early March in North India — called *chūta* in Sanskrit.

NĀGA-KESARA : *Mesua ferrea*, a forest tree of Eastern India with white flowers with yellow interior.

NĀRIKELA : *Cocos nucifera*, the cocoanut palm.

NAVAMALLIKĀ : *Jasminum arborescens*, a shrubby jasmine.

NĪM : *Azadirachta indica*, a shady tree flowering in March-April.

PADAM : *Prunus cerasioides*, wild cherry found in the temperate Himalayas at altitudes from 3,000 to 6,000 feet.

PĀRIJĀTAKA : *Nyctanthes arbortristis*, drops its flowers early in the morning.

PĀṬALA : *Bignonia suaveolens*, trumpet-flower, herald of spring.

PĪPAL : *Ficus religiosa*, a large tree with glossy, dark-green, poplar-like leaves.

PĪTAL : A yellow flower not identified.

PLANTAIN : *Musa paradisiaca, kaila* — smooth straight stem, symbol of female beauty.

PRIYAṄGU : *Panicum italicum*, a shrub flowering in August.

PUNNĀGA : *Calophyllum inophyllum*, a tree with glabrous leaves, and fragrant white flowers.

ŚĀLA : *Shorea robusta*, a tall timber tree, one of the trees associated with the birth of the Buddha.

SAPTACHCHHADA : *Alstonia scholaris*, a handsome tree.

SANDAL : *Santalum album*, a small evergreen tree growing in Mysore, its heart-wood is fragrant. Sandal paste is used in summer for cooling the body.

SARJA (Sk.) : *Shorea robusta*, *Śāla*, a large timber tree.

SARSON : *Brassica campestris*, an oilseed plant with golden yellow flowers.

SEMAL : *Bombax malabaricum*, silk-cotton tree.

ŚĀLMALĪ : *Salmalia malabarica*, silk-cotton tree — beautiful cup-like red flowers in early March.

ŚIRĪSHA : *Albizzia lebeck*, fragrant flowers in early rain.

SĪŚAM : *Dalbergia sissoo*, a deciduous tree with hard wood, principally found in sub-Himalayan areas of North India.

TĀLA : *Borassus flabelliformis*, palmyra — round purple fruits, symbol of female charm.

TAMĀLA : *Garcinia xanthochymus*, or *Cinnamomum tamāla*, straight stem, dark fragrant leaves, symbol of Kṛishṇa.

VAKULA : *Mimusops elengi, moulsari*, a dwarf tree, bears highly fragrant flowers during rains.

YŪTHIKĀ : *Jasminum auriculatum*, a jasmine with fragrant white flowers tinged with purple.

REFERENCES AND NOTES

i. NOGUCHI, Y. *The Spirit of Japanese Poetry*, p. 84.

1. COOMARASWAMY, *Rajput Painting*, p. 42.

2. TOLSTOY thus defines true art: "There is one indubitable indication distinguishing real art from its counterfeit, namely, the infectiousness of art. If a man, without exercising effort and without altering his standpoint, on reading, hearing, or seeing another man's work, experiences a mental condition which unites him with that man and with other people who also partake of that work of art, then the object evoking that condition is a work of art."
"If a man is infected by the author's condition of soul, if he feels this emotion and this union with others, then the object which has effected this is art; but if there be no such infection, if there be not this union with the author and with others who are moved by the same work — then it is not art. And not only is infection a sure sign of art, but the degree of infectiousness is also the sole measure of excellence in art."
TOLSTOY, *What is Art?* pp. 132, 133.

3. STANLEY, *The Beauty of Woman*, p. 119.

4. Quoted by B. S. Mathur in *Homage to Coomaraswamy*, Vol. II, p. 110.

5. PLATO, *Symposium*, *c.* 370 B.C., translated by Robert Bridges in *The Spirit of Man*, 1916.

6. GRIERSON, *The Modern Vernacular Literature of Hindustan*, p. 24.

7. The idea is that the unaesthetic *Nāyaka* has a weakness for the crude *Śaṅkhinī*. Here the banana trees, *champaka* buds, lotus-beds, dates and grapes are symbolic of the refined *Padminī*, *Śaṅkhinī* being her exact anti-thesis.

8. A spell named 'Heart-winning', capable of rendering the three worlds obedient.

9. It is customary in India to look at the crescent of the moon on the second lunar night.

10. Coomaraswamy, in *Rajput Painting*, pp. 45-46, mentions a Pahāṛī drawing of a similar type inscribed with the following verse of Kāli Dās, a Hindi poet, who flourished about 1700 A.D.

"She sits by her husband's side and hears the recital,
her veil and his scarf are knotted together, her eyes cast down,
she never behaves amiss in the eyes of other people!
O Kāli Dās! then comes Govinda to pay a visit, and the beauty
intoxicate with desires, devours him in her longing,—
The shape of that hardy lover remains before her,
she flashes a moment's glance through her veil,—
Go to how is the woman's heart taken up with the new sage,
while the garrulous *purohit* mumbles *Purāṇas*."

The behaviour of *Rādhā* reminds one of the famous Punjabi folk song:

"With the edge of her veil she fanned out the earthen lamp
With the twinkle of her eye she beckoned me."

11. There are a number of paintings showing Kṛishṇa carrying a lotus to Rādhā. When it is a withered lotus, it shows his sadness, and when it is full-blown it shows his joyful heart. Possibly the time of meeting is also indicated, night by a lotus bud, and day by an open flower.

12. The last three categories are according to the poet Sardar given in the *Satsaiyyā* of Bihārī by Grierson, pp. 36 and 37.

13. VIDYĀPATI, *Baṅgīya Padāvalī*, Trans. by Coomaraswamy and Sen, p. 6.

14. Coomaraswamy, *Catalogue of Indian Collection in the Museum of Fine Arts*, Boston, Part V, p. 163.

15. *Ibid.*, p. 203.

16. Quoted by Blyth in *Zen in English Literature*.

17. VIDYĀPATI, *Baṅgīya Padāvalī*, Trans. by Coomaraswamy and Sen, p. 122.

18. *Ibid.*, p. 128.

19. *Ibid.*, p. 116.

20. RICE, *The Seasons and the Labors of the Months in Islamic Art*, *Ars Orientalis*, Vol. I, pp. 2, 3, 8 and 13.

21. An account of twelve months or *Bārāmasā* is often found in the ballads of East Bengal. The description of the twelve months in the ballad of *Dewānā Madīnā* is full of thrilling pathos. The most delightful account of the months is however in the ballad of

Śānti. Śānti was married as a child, and when she comes of age an attractive young man comes to her village and tempts her. The flirtation continues over twelve months, but Śānti remains firm. Ultimately he turns out to be the husband of Śānti. The delightful translation below is by Dineshchandra Sen.

Śānti

(1)

"Sweet October has come, sweet is the milk in unripe *āman* rice. My mind is restless, O Śānti, as I behold thy youthful charms."

"Calm thy restless heart and quiet thy soul, O lad, tomorrow at dawn shall I go to yonder landing-*ghāṭ* all alone and meet you there."

"Neither am I a physician, lad, nor versed in the sacred lore; a simple village girl, daughter of Guno of the Baniya caste am I. If indeed you suffer from a malady, how can I cure it?"

(2)

"You are filling your pitcher, girl, go on doing so. But know that I am in charge of the tank and guard it here."

"False! It is the virtuous king who has dug the tank and made its landing-*ghāṭ* of stone for public use. I, the girl Śānti, am filling my pitcher from the tank. I do not believe thee and care not for any guard."

"You have deceived me, O Śānti, all these days of November by your glib tongue. My hopes have even more remained unfulfilled. Behold with new charms on the landscape, November has made its appearance."

(3)

"In this sweet November thou lookest like a silvery streak of moon-beams; O, do not vanish away, but allow me, a stranger, to be revived by a sight of thee."

"Night is coming. I must take care that my mother-in-law may sleep in comfort. Know me, O youth, to be the darling of my husband. I hold a stranger like you in the light of a father or brother."

"This month, too, thou hast deceived me by your glib tongue. Behold the change on the fair face of Nature, announcing the advent of December."

(4)

"It is December now and hear my vow. I will enter your sleeping room late in the night and get by stealth what I cannot get as a gift."

"A hundred candles will I keep burning in my room to-night, at the gate our elephant, Gajamati, will keep watch."

"I will blow out all your hundred candles, and the elephant Gajamati will I kill at your gate by the force of my arms."

"I will cover my bracelets with the edge of my *sārī* lest they jingle, and, sword in hand, shall I keep watch all night. If, at the end of night, the thief is caught, this is my vow that I shall sacrifice him at the altar of the goddess Chanḍī."

"This month too, Śānti, you have deceived me with your glib tongue. With a change in the landscape has January made its appearance."

(5)

"It is January. Look dear one, the *sārī* you wear is too short. Spread its flowing end as far as you can and receive the humble present of betels and nuts that I have brought for you."

"Take away these presents, I do not want them, lad. You have an elder sister at your house, present these to her, if you like."

"Cruel words hast thou spoken, O Śānti. The presents I mean for you, and you wish them to be given to my sister! You cause pain to my heart by saying so. Now for all these days of January you have played cunningly with me, deferring hopes from day to day. Behold, February shows itself with all its new and beauteous colours in Nature."

(6)

"It is February. The nights are long. If on such a night a guest comes to your door what will you do to receive him?"

"A couch and sofa will be spread for him in the outer room; soft pillows will be given to make his sleep easy and sound. He will have fine rice and pulses for his meals, and blanket will be given him to make the wintry night warm."

"You have beguiled me, dear girl, with your glib tongue this month also. My hopes remain unfulfilled evermore. Behold the approach of March, bringing an array of fresh charms to the landscape around."

(7)

"It is March. The heat is scorching. Thy beauteous and youthful figure, O Śānti, burns my heart with a desire, which I know not how to allay."

"A bad mother gave birth to you, wicked youth, and your father was a wretched eunuch. If there is heat in your body, why not jump down into yonder river and cool your body's heat therein."

"This month is also gone, O Śānti. You have deceived me by your glib tongue and withheld the fulfilment of my hopes. On the fair face of Nature have bloomed forth the new beauties announcing April."

(8)

"It is April now. Like the sweet layer of cream over milk to your lovely youth, O Śānti! but what purpose does it serve, if like a miser, you guard your treasure from others."

"My youth is not a water-melon to be cut to pieces for distribution at dinner. Nor is it the milk of a woman's breast for feeding her babe."

"O cunning one, this month is also gone and you have beguiled me by your glib tongue. I pine with unfulfilled hopes. Behold the new charm of the landscape, indicating the approach of May."

(9)

"It is May. The mangoes are ripe in yonder grove; plenty of these fruits, besides jacks and black-berries, have I brought as my humble present for you."

"Keep these aside. lad, I do not want them. Go home and present them to your sister."

"Cruel are your words, O Śānti, these presents are made to you and you cause pain to my heart by your refusal. This month has also gone and my hopes are evermore deferred. Look at the change of landscape, announcing June."

(10)

"It is June, O Śānti, behold the flood in rivers. Near Kāñchanpur in the swelling stream has your husband been drowned on his way home."

"False! Had my husband died in the swelling stream near Kāñchanpur, the chignon on my head would have been unloose of itself. The pearl-necklace on my breast would have been unstrung, the shell-bracelets in my hands, known by their pet names, Rāma and Lakshmaṇa would have been broken and the brightness of the red sign of luck on my forehead would have slowly faded away. I believe in these signs and not in your reports, O false lad."

"This month, also, hast thou beguiled me by thy glib tongue. My hopes are unfulfilled and I am joyless. Behold, on all sides, July's advent is proclaimed by a change in the landscape."

(11)

"It is July. The muddy knee-deep water is seen everywhere. When passing from one house to another through this watery path, you will be served with some gentle strokes from my stick of twigs as punishment."

"Beat me as hard as you can with your stick, O lad. Kill me and float my body in the river. But know, still I will not go to a stranger's house."

"This month, also, hast thou beguiled me by your glib tongue, and my hopes remain unrealised. Behold, Nature wears a new apparel at the advent of August."

(12)

"It is August. The rivers are full. I will give you a boat rowed by sixteen men for playing race in this pleasing season."

"Give your boat to your sister or to your mother, or to those who care for your presents, I do not value them."

"This month, too, you have beguiled me by your cunning words. Nature now has changed her scenes and announces September."

(13)

It is September. In every house the divine mother Durgā is worshipped.

"Look at me closely, O Śānti, I am here, thy own dear husband, returned home after long days. Don't you know me dear?"

Śānti bowed her head down at these words. "Swear by God" she said "and speak the truth."

"Which is your native city? What is your name, O youth? And who are your parents?"

"I am a native of Bāhātiā. There I own a house of my own. My father is a Kalpataru and my mother's name is Gaṇeśvarī. I married you, O Śānti, years ago, on the fifteenth of an October. The pet name by which I am called, is Killan Sadāgar."

"If really art thou the dear one of my heart, be pleased to stay here a while. I will return instantly after enquiring of my parents if your account is true."

(14)

"O, my old father, and O, my dear mother, what are you busy with, at this moment? Will you tell me to whom you have given me, your daughter?"

"You have passed your twelfth year, and now stand on the threshold of youth. Is it the inclination, natural to your age, that makes you discover a husband at the gate?"

With a lamp in hand and a *toka* on his head, the old man walks in slow pace to see if really the son-in-law has come.

"It is he, O Śānti, no doubt, it is he. Go, receive him. He, the jewel of your heart, has been found at last. Now open the chest, containing your dresses and ornaments. Find out your hair-comb of mica and articles of toilet."

Śānti divided her hair into two lovely rows and made a chignon, over which she spread garlands of *champā* and *pārul* flowers. She put a tiara on her head and wore the *chandanahāra* and a waist-belt of the moon-pattern. From her neck hung a lovely necklace. She wore armlets on her arms and bracelets on her wrist. Anklets jingled on her feet and a string of the largest pearls she wore on her breast. Her eyes she beautified with black *kājal* dye, and to finish all, she put, on her forehead, the red mark of luck.

See how bright and lovely she looks to-night, as she softly treads the ground to go to the nuptial room to receive the husband of her heart.

—Eastern Bengal Ballads, Vol II: Part-I, pp. 123-128

22. The Hindu months and their English equivalents are :—

Chaitra, March-April; *Baisākha*, April-May;
Jyeshṭha, May-June; *Āshāḍha*, June-July;
Śrāvaṇa, July-August; *Bhādon*, August-September;
Āśvina (Āsoja), September-October; *Kārttika*, October-November;
Agahana, November-December; *Pausha*, December-January;
Māgha, January-February; *Phālguna*, February-March.

23. Sanskrit poets had a number of women and tree legends. It was said that the *aśoka* flowered when its roots were pressed by the feet of a lovely woman, the *kurabaka* when embraced by her, the *priyaṅgu* by contact with her, the *vakula* when sprayed with a mouthful of wine, the *mandāra* by her soft caressing words, the *champaka* by her winsome smile, the mango by her balmy breath, and the *karṇikāra* by her dance.

24. Laurence Binyon, *The Spirit of Man in Asian Art*, p. 141.

25. VIDYĀPATI, *Baṅgīya Padāvalī*, Trans. by Coomaraswamy and Sen, p. 60.

26. This painting from the collection of the Raja of Lambagraon is an early 19th century example of Kangra art in its last phase at Tira-Sujanpur, and was possibly painted under the patronage of Aniruddha Chand. The *nāyaka* resembles Aniruddha Chand. Patrons of paintings were often accepted as models by the Kangra artists, and shown as heroes.

27. VIDYĀPATI, *Baṅgīya Padāvalī*, Trans. by Coomaraswamy and Sen, p. 12.

28. A crow is the symbol of separated lovers. When a crow is cawing on the cornice of a house, the wife separated from her husband, asks him to fly away and to bring the news of her dear one. A crow cawing is regarded as an omen of a guest arriving.

29. The linear cypresses alternating with mangoes shown in this painting is a convention of the Guler artists. It bears an inscription in Gurmukhi script on the top. It was most likely executed by a Guler artist for a Sikh patron, probably Maharaja Sher Singh, son of Maharaja Ranjit Singh, who was very fond of Kangra hills, and had even married a hill woman.

30. POWYS MATHERS, *Love Songs of Asia*, p. 63.

31. The Hindi Śṛiṅgāra literature both in Sanskrit and Hindi has its roots in Bharata's *Nāṭyaśāstra*, a treatise on dramaturgy. Poetry, music, and dance were necessary components of Hindu drama, and as such the book also deals with poetics, music and the language of gesture. According to Manomohan Ghosh, the available text of the *Nāṭyaśāstra* existed in the second century A.D., while the tradition which it recorded may go back to a period as early as 100 B.C. It is composed mainly in verse in the form of a dialogue between Bharata and some ancient sages. Apart from Sanskrit, the *Nāṭyaśāstra* also gives examples of Prākṛit verses. It is the earliest writing on poetics, contains discussions on figures of speech (*alaṁkāra*), mentions ten qualities and faults of a composition and describes 58 varieties of metre. In relation to *ars amatoria* it mentions the *Kāmatantra* and the *Kāma-śāstra*, but there is no reference to Vātsyāyana's *Kāmasūtra*, which was composed much later.

The *Nāṭyaśāstra* expounds the doctrine of sentiment or *rasa*, and emotional states or *bhāvas*. It further describes the emotions of women or *hāvas*, followed by a classification of ten stages of a woman's love. Then the eight-fold classification of *nāyikās* is given. Female messengers, their qualities and functions, and the meeting places of lovers are mentioned, followed by an account of *māna*, and the methods adopted to overcome it.

This elaborate classification of man and woman according to moods, sentiments, and situations was developed mainly as an aid to dramatic art. After describing the emotions and emotional states, the *Nāṭyaśāstra* mentions the facial expressions and gestures appropriate to the particular situations which the actors and actresses should practise. Ghosh observes, "The *Nāṭyaśāstra* seems to be the first in recognizing the two-fold importance of psychology in connexion with the production of a play. Its classification of heroes and heroines according to their typical mental and emotional states proves its admission of the importance of psychology on the creative side of the dramatic art; for with the complete knowledge of all possible reactions of different objects and incidents upon such heroes and heroines, the play-wright as well as actors and actresses could attain the greatest possible success in characterisation. On the critical side also the importance of psychology was discovered by the Hindu theorists almost simultaneously. It was realised that no strictly objective standard of beauty ever existed, and the enjoyment of a theatrical production consisted of peculiar reactions which the art of the play-wright as well as that of the actors could successfully evoke in spectators of different types. It is on this assumption that the theory of sentiments and states has been elaborated by the author of the *Nāṭyaśāstra*."

It would be seen that the entire theme of *nāyikā-bheda* as elaborated by Keshav Dās is already present in the *Nāṭyaśāstra*. There is elaboration in respect of certain features, e.g. the classification of *nāyakas* and *nāyikās* as given in Chapter II of this book. The main contribution of Keshav Dās, however, is in the examples which he has given to illustrate the various heroes, heroines, situations, and sentiments. In these examples the *nāyaka* is Kṛishṇa, and the *nāyikā* is Rādhā, while *sakhīs* intervene to reconciliate, to remove misunderstanding, and ultimately bring them together. While in the *Nāṭyaśāstra* classification of man and his mental and physical traits, and moods is more elaborate, as it was necessary for the purposes of drama, in the *Rasikapriyā* the emphasis was mainly on woman, who is certainly more interesting and more complex than man. The theme of *Nāyikā-bheda* was developed for the instruction of princes and nobles in the art of love, and also for propagating the new religion of *bhakti* which emerged in the form of Rādhā-Kṛishṇa cult.

BIBLIOGRAPHY

ARCHER, W. G. *Kangra Painting*, London 1952.
—— *Indian Painting in the Punjab Hills*, London 1952.
—— *The Loves of Krishna*, London 1957.
—— *Indian Painting*, London 1957.
—— *Indian Miniatures*, New York 1960.
ASHTA, D. P. *The Poetry of the Dasam Granth*, New Delhi 1959.
BINYON, Laurence. *The Spirit of Man in Asian Art*, Cambridge, Massachusetts 1935.
BLYTH, R. H. *Zen in English Literature*, Tokyo 1942.
COOMARASWAMY, A. K. *Indian Drawings*, London 1910-12.
—— *Rajput Painting*, 2 Vols., Oxford 1916.
—— *Catalogue of the Indian Collections in the Museum of Fine Arts*, Boston 1926.
——* *The Eight Nāyikās*, Journal of Indian Art and Industry, Vol. 16, No. 128, 1914.
——* *Two Leaves from a Seventeenth-Century Manuscript of the Rasikapriyā* (Metropolitan Museum Studies—Vol. III, Pt. I — Dec., 1930).
EASTMAN, A. C. *The Nala Damayanti Drawings*, Museum of Fine Arts, Boston 1959.
FRENCH, J. C. *Himalayan Art*, London 1931.
GANGOLY, O. C. *Masterpieces of Rajput Painting*, Calcutta 1926.
GRIERSON, G. A. *The Modern Vernacular Literature of Hindustan*, Calcutta 1889.
GHOSH, M. *The Nāṭyaśāstra*, Calcutta 1951.
KĀLIDĀSA *The Ṛitusaṁhāra*, edited by L. S. Fansikar, Bombay 1900.
KESHAV DĀS *Kavipriyā*, with commentary by L. N. Chaturvedi, Allahabad 1952.
—— *Rasikapriyā*, with commentary by Visvanathprasad Misra, Varanasi, Saṁvat 2015.
KHANDALAVALA, K. *Pahari Miniature Painting*, Bombay 1958.
MATHERS, E. POWYS (Trans.) *Love Songs of Asia*, London 1944.
MEHTA, N. C. *Studies in Indian Painting*, Bombay 1926.
NOGUCHI, Y. *The Spirit of Japanese Poetry*, London 1914.
PADAM, P. S. *Punjabi Baramahen* (in Punjabi), Patiala 1959.
PLATO *Symposium*, *c.* 370 B.C., translated by Robert Bridges in '*The Spirit of Man*,' London 1916.
RANDHAWA, M. S. **Kangra Paintings illustrating the life of Shiva and Parvati*, Roopa-Lekhā, Vol. 24, 1953.
——* *Guler, the Birthplace of Kangra Art*, Marg, Vol. VI, No. 4, 1953.
——* *Sujanpur Tira, the Cradle of Kangra Art*, Marg, Vol. VII, No. 3, 1953.
——* *Kangra Valley School of Painting*, Art & Letters, 28 : 1-9, 1954.
——* *Moonlight in Kangra Paintings*, March of India, March-April, 1954.
—— *Kangra Valley Painting*, New Delhi 1954.
——* *Kangra Paintings on Love*, Studio, Sept., 1954.
——* *Some Nurpur Paintings*, Marg, Vol. VIII, No. 3, June, 1955.
——* *Kangra Artists*, Art and Letters, 29 : 1-9, 1955.
——* *Paintings from Nālāgrah*, Lalit Kalā Nos. 1-2, 1956.
—— *The Krishna Legend*, Lalit Kalā Akademi, New Delhi 1956.
——* *A Journey to Basohli*, Roopa-Lekhā, Vol. XXVIII, 1958.
——* *Kangra Rāgamālā Paintings*, Roopa-Lekhā, Vol. XXIX, 1958.
——* *Some inscribed Pahārī paintings with names of artists*, Roopa-Lekhā, Vol. XXX, No. 1, 1959.
——* *Was Manak, the painter of Gīta Govinda paintings, a Garhwal artist?* Roop-Lekhā, Vol. XXXI, No. 1, 1960.
——* *Paintings from Mankot*, Lalit Kalā, No. 6, 1959.
—— *Basohli Painting*, Publications Division, Ministry of Information and Broadcasting, Government of India, New Delhi 1959.
—— *Kangra Paintings of the Bhāgavata Purāṇa*, National Museum, New Delhi 1960.
REIFF, R. *Indian Miniatures, the Rajput Painters*, Tokyo, Rutland and Vermont, 1959.
RICE, D. S. **The Seasons and the Labors of Months in Islamic Art*, Ars Orientalis, Vol. I, 1954.
SEN, D. *Eastern Bengal Ballads*, Vol. II, Part I, Calcutta 1926.
SINGAM, S. D. R. *Homage to Ananda Coomaraswamy*, Vol. II, Kuantan, Malaya 1952.
STANLEY LOUIS *The Beauty of Woman*, London 1955.
TOLSTOY, L. N. *The Kingdom of God is Within You, What is Art ? What is Religion ?* New York 1899.
VIDYĀPATI *Baṅgīya Padāvalī* — Songs of the Love of Rādhā and Kṛishṇa; translated into English by A. K. Coomaraswamy and Arun Sen, London 1915.

Note : Publications marked with asterisks are papers and others are books.

INDEX

INDEX